100 MOST UNEXPLAINED

MYSTERIES ON THE PLANET

Quarto is the authority on a wide range of topics.

Quarto educates, entertains and enriches the lives of our readers—enthusiasts and lovers of hands-on living.

www.quartoknows.com

Published in the UK in 2016 by QED Publishing

ISBN 978-1-78493-725-6

Publisher: Zeta Jones
Art Director: Susi Martin
Designer: Dave and Angela Ball
Production: Nikki Ingram

Printed and bound in China by Toppan Leefung Printers Ltd.

10 9 8 7 6 5 4 3 2 1   16 17 18 19 20

100 MOST UNEXPLAINED
MYSTERIES ON THE PLANET

CONTENTS

6   Introduction

8-9   Yeti • Bigfoot
10-11   Loch Ness monster • Lake Champlain monster
12-13   Bunyip • Kraken
14-15   Dingonek • Minhocão
16-17   Mongolian death worm • Orang pendek
18-19   Mothman • Mermaids
20-21   Bermuda Triangle • Sailing stones
22-23   Taos hum • Giant footprint
24-25   Nan Madol • Skeleton Lake
26-27   Stonehenge • Göbekli Tepe
28-29   Atlantis • Yonaguni Monument
30-31   Costa Rica stone spheres • Nazca lines
32-33   Walls of Saksaywaman • Easter Island statues
34-35   Pyramids of Giza • The Sphinx
36-37   Saqqara Bird • Baigong pipes
38-39   Antikythera mechanism • Baghdad batteries
40-41   Oakville blobs • Star jelly
42-43   Ball lightning • Flying saucer clouds
44-45   Red rain of Kerala • Animal rain
46-47   Earthquake lights • Naga fireballs
48-49   Paulding light • Crop circles
50-51   Out-of-body experiences • Sliders
52-52   Psychokinesis • Telepathy
54-55   ESP • Spontaneous human combustion
56-57   Borley Rectory • The Brown Lady of Raynham Hall
58-59   Myrtles Plantation • Rose Hall
60-61   The Stanley Hotel • Winchester Mystery House

62-63	Abraham Lincoln • The Flying Dutchman
64-65	Theatre Royal ghost • Tower of London ghosts
66-67	Glamis Castle • Ballygally Castle
68-69	Edinburgh Vaults • Knighton Gorges Manor
70-71	Faces of Belmez • Faces of SS Watertown
72-73	Amelia Earhart • Flight 19
74-75	Mary Celeste • Eilean Mòr mystery
76-77	Phineas Gage • Fabrice Muamba
78-79	Vesna Vulovic • Juliane Koepcke
80-81	Harrison Okene • Paul Templer
82-83	Lubbock lights • Westall landing
84-85	Belgian UFO wave • Roswell incident
86-87	Betty and Barney Hill • Allagash abductions
88-89	Linda Napolitano • Rendlesham Forest UFO
90-91	Linear A • Rongorongo
92-93	Voynich manuscript • Rohonc codex
94-95	Wow! signal • Moon illusion
96-97	Placebo effect • Déjà vu
98-99	Why do we yawn? • Why do we dream?
100-101	Origin of life • Life on other planets
102-103	Monarch migrations • Periodical cicadas
104-105	Gravity • Matter
106-107	Time • Consciousness
108-109	Glossary
110-111	Index
112	Acknowledgements

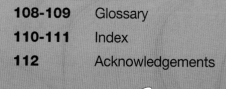

INTRODUCTION

We humans like to think we are an advanced, hi-tech civilization who understand most of the things around us. We've invented computers, split the atom, developed life-saving medicines, and built flying machines. Thousands of scientists all over the world are constantly studying our planet and learning more and more about how everything works. We've explained pretty much everything there is to explain – right?

WRONG! The amount of stuff we don't yet understand and haven't yet explained is mind-boggling. It ranges from mysterious animal behaviour to what happens in our own brains, and from ancient writing we still can't decode to the mystery of what everything is actually made of. What is time? Do aliens exist? What are dreams for? And is the Mongolian death worm a real creature? To these and many other very important questions, we have to admit that our answer is – we don't really know!

PARANORMAL PUZZLES

Millions of people are absolutely convinced that things like ghosts, telepathy and out-of-body experiences – known as the paranormal – are real. Many ghosts, for example, have been reported by numerous different witnesses. But when science tries to prove these things, they turn out to be strangely difficult to pin down. This book explores some of the most famous paranormal claims, to see if they could be true.

ANCIENT SECRETS

Humans have been building, inventing, and creating things for many thousands of years, but often, all that remains of ancient civilizations is a handful of clues. The things they left behind, like Stonehenge, or the ancient writing system Linear A, hold unexplained mysteries that experts are still trying to solve.

MYSTERIES OF SCIENCE

Science might seem factual and straightforward, but actually, the opposite is true. The more scientists study things like time, gravity, matter, and the brain, the more they realize that we are far from explaining any of them! At the end of this book, you can find out about some of the mysteries surrounding the everyday things we take for granted.

UNEXPLAINED FACTOR

Each topic in this book has its own unexplained rating.

[?] Not quite as strange as it seems

[?][?] A bit puzzling...

[?][?][?] Curiouser and curiouser...

[?][?][?][?] That's really weird!

[?][?][?][?][?] Mind-bogglingly mysterious!!!

YETI

What if you were in the mountains when a huge, hairy, human-like creature came trudging towards you? It might be a yeti! This wild human is said to live in the Himalayas in Asia, the world's highest mountain range.

We have seen it!

For hundreds of years, local people in China, Nepal and Russia have told tales of the 'wild man'. In the 1900s, mountaineers from other countries began exploring the Himalayas – and several of them reported seeing a tall, hairy, two-legged wild creature. Many more said they had seen giant footprints in the snow.

▶ Reports and photos of yeti footprints suggest they are bigger than human feet, and extremely wide.

Abominable!

The Yeti is also known as the 'abominable snowman', a nickname that dates from 1920s news reports. Because of this, cartoon images often show it with snowy-white fur. But most reports say its fur is actually dark, making it look a bit like a tall gorilla.

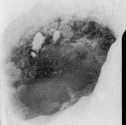

CRYPTO-CREATURES

The Yeti is one of the world's most famous 'cryptids'. Cryptids are unexplained creatures that have not yet been proved to exist. They could be nothing more than myths or made-up stories – or they could be real. The study of cryptids is called 'cryptozoology'.

UNEXPLAINED FACTOR

It's never been proved, but several scientists think the Yeti might really be out there!

BIGFOOT

In the forests and mountains of Canada and North America, there have been sightings of a creature very like the yeti. It's called Bigfoot, or the Sasquatch, and like the yeti it's a big, hairy, human-shaped animal that walks on two legs.

Stinky Sasquatch!

People who claim to have seen Bigfoot often say it had a strong, horrible smell. It's also described as having long hair, a pointy head and big, dark eyes. Some eyewitnesses said it was up to 2.5 metres (8 feet) tall and left footprints 60 centimetres (2 feet) long!

◀ Bigfoot's huge, heavy, hairy body and long arms are often described by witnesses.

UNEXPLAINED FACTOR

There's quite a lot of evidence that Bigfoot might exist, though it's still uncertain.

Caught on camera?

In 1967, film-makers, Roger Patterson and Robert Gimlin, set out to find Bigfoot in Northern California, USA. They claimed they had spotted one and managed to film the creature striding away from the camera. Though some say it's a fake, no one has been able to recreate it convincingly using a costume.

▶ Bigfoot as it appears in the Patterson-Gimlin film.

LOCH NESS MONSTER

Perhaps the best-loved of all cryptids is 'Nessie' – the Loch Ness monster. Reports of a creature in this deep lake in Scotland began at least 1500 years ago. Since then, there have been many eyewitness accounts, and a few hoaxes too... but no one can be sure the monster doesn't exist.

▶ Eyewitness reports often mention a long neck and head above the suface of the water.

MONSTER SPOTTERS

When Columba, an early saint, came to Scotland in the 600s, he's said to have seen a "ferocious monster" in the loch. It grabbed one of his servants, but Columba ordered it to stop – and since then, it's never been known to eat anyone! Witnesses often report a black, smooth shape moving through the water.

UNEXPLAINED FACTOR

If Nessie does exist, it's hard to believe we wouldn't have some proper proof by now.

⁇ ⁇ ⁇ ⁇

HUMPS AND FLIPPERS

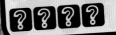

Nessie is often described as having a long neck and a small head, a back with one or more rounded humps, and sometimes flipper-like feet. This would make it very similar to prehistoric water reptiles called plesiosaurs. Could a plesiosaur species have survived, and still be living in the loch?

◀ The Loch Ness monster is often reported as looking like a plesiosaur.

LAKE CHAMPLAIN MONSTER

Lake Champlain, in the northeastern USA, is home to a monster known as 'Champ'. The Iroquois and Abenaki peoples who originally lived there had their own legends about the beast, and left food on the shore for it.

SOUND OF A MONSTER?

In 2003, researchers at the lake recorded underwater sounds similar to the echolocation noises orcas and dolphins make to find their way around. There are no whales or dolphins in the lake – so maybe the monster uses a form of echolocation itself.

UNEXPLAINED FACTOR

Experts think Sandra Mansi's photo is not a fake. Could the monster be real!?

THE SHERIFF'S SIGHTING

In 1873, boat passengers claimed they had crashed into the monster. In 1883, local sheriff Nathan Mooney reported seeing an "enormous snake or water serpent" around 10 metres (30 feet) long, with its head and neck sticking out of the water. He said it was so close he could see it had white spots inside its mouth!

◄ Champ is reported to have a massive snake-like head.

SANDRA MANSI'S STORY

The most famous Champ sighting of all came in 1977, when Sandra Mansi said she saw the water rippling and swirling, then a huge, snake-like head and neck rising above the surface. She managed to snap one photo before running away.

► One of the best lake monster photos ever taken – Sandra Mansi's 1977 Champ snap.

BUNYIP

A 'bunyip' sounds cuddly, doesn't it? But if you lived in Australia a few hundred years ago, the idea of a bunyip was frightening. Basically, it was a fierce water animal that could leap out of ponds or swamps and claw or crush people to death.

BUNYIP BODY PARTS

When Europeans settled in Australia from about 1800, they learned about the bunyip from the Aboriginal people. According to various reports, the creature had thick legs or flippers, bulging eyes, a scaly or furry body shaped like a crocodile's, and a bird's head with a long, tooth-filled beak. Bizarre!

▲ The bunyip was said to wait in ambush near swamps, riverbeds and waterholes.

REAL RIVER MONSTERS

Fossils show that big, strange creatures did live in Australia in prehistoric times. *Diprotodon*, for example, was the biggest ever marsupial (related to kangaroos and koalas) and looked a bit like a huge, fierce hippo. It became extinct around 40,000 years ago – the same time as the Aborigines first came to Australia. Maybe old stories about it, combined with *Diprotodon* skeletons, gave rise to the bunyip.

UNEXPLAINED FACTOR

Surely nothing this weird could really exist. If it did, or does – what is it!?

? ? ? ? ?

KRAKEN

For hundreds of years, sailors told tales of the Kraken – a giant sea monster with huge eyes and many writhing arms. Some said it was so big, its powerful tentacles could reach up, wrap themselves around a ship, and drag it under the waves.

MONSTER MOLLUSC

In the 1700s and 1800s, scientists decided the kraken must be a kind of sea mollusc – an enormous octopus or squid. The reports of large eyes match the squid – big squids like the giant and colossal squid have the largest eyes of any animal. Giant squid are also known to fight sperm whales, so perhaps a big squid might mistake a boat's underside for its whale enemy.

◄ In paintings and drawings, the kraken looks like a massive octopus.

MASSIVE BLOB

In 1896, a giant blob, resembling an octopus's head and body, washed ashore in Florida, USA. Some scientists said it was a dead octopus, missing its tentacles – and when alive, it would have measured up to 30 metres (100 feet) long. However, others thought it was part of a dead whale. We're still waiting for more evidence.

UNEXPLAINED FACTOR

Was the kraken really a giant monster of the sea? Or a giant squid or colossal octopus?

?? ??

DINGONEK

The Dingonek is said to inhabit the rivers of central Africa, devouring anyone who tries to go swimming or fishing in its territory. Because of its two long tusks, it's also called the 'jungle walrus'.

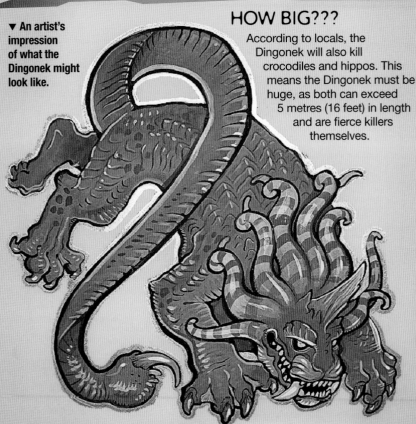

▼ An artist's impression of what the Dingonek might look like.

HOW BIG???

According to locals, the Dingonek will also kill crocodiles and hippos. This means the Dingonek must be huge, as both can exceed 5 metres (16 feet) in length and are fierce killers themselves.

EYEWITNESS ACCOUNT

Explorer John Alfred Jordan claimed to have seen the beast in the early 1900s. Jordan said the 3-metre (14-foot) long Dingonek he met had a leopard-like head with two long fangs and a spotty back. But instead of fur, it had scaly skin, clawed feet like a lizard's and a whale-like tail for swimming.

SABRE-TOOTHED SEAL?

Similar 'water lions' or 'water leopards' have been reported in other parts of Africa too. One strange theory is that the prehistoric sabre-toothed tiger could have survived there, and evolved (gradually changed) into a fierce river animal.

MINHOCÃO

We know that worms burrow through the soil beneath our feet – but they're only small! In Brazil, the Minhocão, if it ever existed, is the biggest burrower of them all. It's a giant worm, at least 1 metre (3 feet) thick, and up to 46 metres (150 feet) long, with a mouth and two horns on its head!

▼ The giant worm-like creature was said to produce enormous trenches as it burrowed.

WORD OF THE WORM

In the 1800s, explorers in South America began writing articles about the Minhocão, based on reports from local people. They described how the worm's burrowing could uproot trees and leave slither-shaped trenches in the soil.

UNEXPLAINED FACTOR

Whether it's a reptile, worm, fish or a millipede – could any of them really grow THIS big?

? ? ? ?

WORM ROAD

Though there were many sightings of the Minhocão in the past, reports have become much rarer. However, the creature is still well known in Brazil. Today, a huge, snake-like superhighway that winds through the city of São Paulo is nicknamed the Mincohão.

WATER WORM

Besides its burrowing habits, the Minhocão was said to love water. Farmers claimed it would lie in wait in a river, then snatch and eat cows and horses that came too close! Because of this, some experts say the Minhocão could be a type of giant caecilian – worm-shaped reptiles that can both burrow and swim.

MONGOLIAN DEATH WORM

Its name sounds like something from a sci-fi film, and its deadly powers are even harder to believe. But ask any Mongolian, and they'll tell you all about the death worm – what it looks like, where it lives, and the horrible things it can do to you.

▼ The vast Gobi Desert, home of the Mongolian death worm.

SPOTTER'S GUIDE

The worm has been described in detail many times. Here are its key features:

- Bright red, sausage-shaped body, wrinkled but not scaly, with dark blotches.
- 60–150 centimetres (2–5 feet) long, with spikes or horns at each end.
- Lives in Mongolia's Gobi Desert, especially around yellow-flowered saxaul bushes.
- Burrows underground, but may surface in warm, damp weather.
- Can kill by squirting venom, or by giving an electric shock!

▼ Artists' impression.

CAMEL KILLER

Locals claim the worms have killed countless people, and even camels, with their deadly shocks and venom. This sounds extreme, but there are animals like electric eels that give electric shocks, and snakes such as the spitting cobra that spit venom. One thing's certain: if you do ever find a Mongolian death worm, you should run!

UNEXPLAINED FACTOR

The worm could be a real animal, still unknown to scientists – though it may not be as deadly as claimed.

ANIMAL ATTRACTION
Don't wear a yellow T-shirt in the Gobi Desert. The death worm is said to be especially attracted to yellow!

ORANG PENDEK

You've probably heard of the orangutan – an ape from the jungles of Southeast Asia. Its name means 'person of the forest', though it's not human. Locals also talk of the 'orang pendek', meaning 'small person' – and this one is much more like a human. Scientists have tried to find it, but its existence is still a mystery.

◄ The orang pendek walks upright and has a strong chest and arms.

SMALL BUT STRONG

Most reports of the orang pendek come from the island of Sumatra, part of Indonesia. For hundreds of years, local people and visitors have reported seeing a human-like, but very small creature in the forest. It is said to stand about 90 centimetres (3 feet) tall, with short brown hair all over its body, and longer hair, like a human's, on its head.

UNEXPLAINED FACTOR

There are so many reports, this is starting to look quite believable!

FAMILY MEMBER?

In 2003, scientists found fossils of an extinct species of small human – Flores Man – on the Indonesian island of Flores. This shows tiny humans did exist in the area. Could the orang pendek be related to them?

MOTHMAN

Some cryptids are only seen for a short time, then disappear – like the strange and spooky Mothman, of West Virginia, USA. Many witnesses spotted this mysterious flying creature during 1966 and 1967, around the town of Point Pleasant.

WHAT WAS IT LIKE?

Mothman was described as being as tall as a man, with huge wings and bright red eyes. It was seen flying low over the ground, following cars, or perching on buildings. And in some cases, pet dogs vanished, never to be seen again!

IS IT A BIRD?

Some experts think Mothman was a very big bird. Suggestions include the sandhill crane and the eagle owl, which both have broad wingspans and red eyes. Fear and darkness might have confused witnesses.

◄ In the dark, a bird like this might look like a red-eyed, flying human figure.

MORE MOTHMEN?

In December 1967, a disaster struck Point Pleasant when the nearby Silver Bridge collapsed. After that, Mothman sightings stopped. However, Mothman-like beings have popped up in various parts of the world since then. One, known as the Owlman, briefly appeared in a village in Cornwall, UK, in the 1970s.

◄ The people of Point Pleasant remember their Mothman with a silvery statue.

MERMAIDS

Mermaids appear in myths and artworks from all over the world, dating back 3000 years. There are also real-life reports from people who believe they've seen them, including the pirate Blackbeard, and the explorer Christopher Columbus.

▼ A mermaid with the upper body of a female human and the tail of a fish.

MERMAID SIGHTINGS

During the Second World War, a soldier stationed on an island in Indonesia said he saw locals catch a pinkish-skinned mermaid in a fishing net. Meanwhile, soldiers on the nearby Kei islands said they saw 'sea people' also with pink skin, but with arms and legs and spiny heads, which the locals called *orang ikan* or 'fishman'.

TAIL OR NO TAIL?

In both legends and sightings, there are two kinds of mermaids. Some look like a fish from the waist down, while others look human, but have webbed hands and feet, fishy faces and often a crest of spines on their heads.

◀ Some mermaid sightings could have actually been manatees or seals.

UNEXPLAINED FACTOR

They seem magical and impossible, but the sea is so huge, it's possible mermaids might exist....

? ? ? ?

BERMUDA TRIANGLE

The Bermuda Triangle is an area of the Atlantic Ocean famous for its disappearances. Dozens of boats and planes have met a watery end on their way through the triangle, some of them vanishing forever without a trace. What happened to them?

UNEXPLAINED FACTOR

This terrifying triangle is not actually as strange as it might seem.

ISLE OF DEVILS

Even hundreds of years ago, sailors knew the waters around Bermuda were dangerous – they called it the 'Isle of Devils'. After a number of unexplained 20th century disasters, magazines began publishing articles about the 'sea mystery' in the area, and in 1964 the name 'Bermuda Triangle' was born. Theories to explain the mystery have included alien abductions, sea monsters or even mysterious portals into space!

But the truth is probably a bit more boring. The Bermuda Triangle has many shallow reefs, rocky islands, and frequent deadly hurricanes – as well as a lot of sea and air traffic. Ships and planes do go missing, but that happens in other places too. In fact, statistics show several areas of the world's seas and oceans are even MORE dangerous. They are just not as busy or as well-known.

Bermuda ▶

Miami ▶

Bermuda Triangle

Puerto Rico ▶

▲ The Bermuda Triangle isn't a real thing – it's a triangle-shaped area usually said to lie between Miami, Florida, USA, and the islands of Bermuda and Puerto Rico.

DEADLY DISASTER

One of the deadliest Bermuda Triangle disasters was the disappearance of a ship, the USS Cyclops, in 1918, carrying a cargo of mineral ore and 306 passengers and crew. None of them were ever seen again.

SAILING STONES

If you left a large rock on a flat piece of ground, you'd expect it to stay there. But at Racetrack Playa, a completely flat, dried-out lake bed in California, USA, there are rocks that wander around.
BY THEMSELVES!

TRACKS IN THE MUD

The rocks are known as the sailing stones. For over 100 years, people have been observing and measuring their slow movements. Each stone also leaves a trail in the dry mud, revealing its path. But no one has ever seen the stones in motion!

UP OR DOWN?

One theory claimed the rocks were simply gradually slipping downhill. The lake bed was measured, and it was found to have a very shallow slope – but in the other direction! The rocks actually slide very slightly uphill.

▼ Some of the rocks are huge – far too big for a human to lift!

MUD, WATER AND ICE

Geologists have different theories to explain the mystery. The playa floods with shallow water, making it muddy. Some believe wind could blow the stones along the slippery mud. Others say it happens when the water freezes, making ice sheets that slide around and carry the stones with them. So far, the scientists can't agree.

UNEXPLAINED FACTOR

There must be an explanation. But we don't know what it is!

❓❓❓❓

21

TAOS HUM

In Taos in New Mexico, USA, many people have reported hearing a strange sound, described as a buzz or a rumbling noise. While some hear nothing, for others the sound is so annoying it stops them from sleeping. The hum is often louder at night, and easier to hear when you are indoors.

WHAT IS IT?

Some have blamed the hum on military equipment, others have suggested it could be caused by earth tremors. However, there are no reports of hums from before 1940. This suggests they could be to do with industrial machines, power stations or electrical wiring.

UNEXPLAINED FACTOR

Many people have reported hearing the Taos hum. But could it be caused by heavy industry?

? ? ? ?

◄ The hum is said to be more audible indoors.

RECORDING THE HUM

It's often hard to record the sound of a hum – even when hearers say it's there, microphones don't pick it up. But in 2006, a scientist in New Zealand, using super-sensitive equipment, managed to record what could be a hum. It's a quiet sound at a frequency of about 60Hz – as deep as a very low male voice.

HUM HEARERS

Taos has the most famous hum, but they have also been reported in England, Scotland and Australia. Wherever the hum happens, only a proportion of the population notice it. These select few are sometimes called 'hearers' or 'hummers'.

GIANT FOOTPRINT

What would you think if you came across a giant human footprint in solid stone? In Mpumalanga, South Africa, there is a footprint about 1.2 metres (4 feet) long. To have feet that big, a human being would have to be around 7 or 8 metres (25 feet) tall!

IS IT REAL?

The footprint is there, and it looks as if it was made by a giant foot. Some people believe it's evidence that giants once walked the Earth. They say that after the footprint was made, movements of the Earth's crust pushed the rock into its upright position.

◀ The footprint is in basalt rock.

▶ Average human footprint.

BUT HANG ON...

Scientists have pointed out that the rock is basalt, formed from magma (molten rock). So the giant must have trod in sizzling hot lava – yeeouch! The rock is also billions of years old, and fossils suggest there were no mammals at all then, let alone humans. It's likely the footprint formed by erosion, and just happens to be foot-shaped.

HOW BIG CAN A HUMAN BE?

There is some fossil evidence that extra-tall humans once lived on Earth, but only up to about 2.5 metres (8 feet) tall. In fact, humans 7–8 metres (25 feet) tall wouldn't be able to walk, because they couldn't support their own weight.

UNEXPLAINED FACTOR

We don't actually know who or what made the footprint – but it probably wasn't a giant!

NAN MADOL

The Pacific island of Pohnpei has a very unusual ancient ruin – instead of standing on land, it was built in the sea! The strange city of Nan Madol was created for Pohnpei's chiefs to live on, and as a place for religious ceremonies and burials.

BASALT COLUMNS

The islands and their walls are mostly built of basalt columns – long, tube-shaped, multi-sided 'sticks' of rock that form from volcanic lava. They are great for building strong walls, but heavy – some are 4.5 metres (15 feet) long and weigh up to 5000 kilograms (11,000 pounds) – as much as an elephant!

BUILDING ISLANDS

Pohnpei is surrounded by coral reefs, so the sea around it is quite shallow. Nan Madol is made up of 92 artificial islands built on the reef. The ancient builders, who started work around the year 1200, somehow carried thousands of boulders and stone columns out into the sea to construct the islands.

▼ In this picture you can see the neat, criss-crossing pattern of stones the builders used to make the strong island walls.

UNEXPLAINED FACTOR

No one knows exactly how this amazing feat was achieved. It must have taken ages!

❓❓❓

Local stories say that the rulers who built Nan Madol were not native islanders – they arrived from far away and were cruel and very tall. According to legend, they moved the stones for the islands with the help of a flying dragon and a magic spell that made the stones float through the air. Handy!

▲ Nan Madol is very overgrown today, but this map shows its layout clearly.

SKELETON LAKE

5000 metres (16,500 feet) up in the Indian Himalayas lies a shallow lake that spends most of the year frozen. But when it melts, for just a month or two every summer, up to 200 skeletons are revealed lying around the lake's edges and under the shallow water. Spooooky!

WHO DIED HERE?

Locals have always known about the bones, but in 1942, the lake became better known after a forest ranger came across the skeletons. Some claimed the bones came from an ancient battle, or a group of travellers ambushed by enemies or caught in a landslide.

LEAVE THOSE BONES ALONE!

Many trekkers and tourists visit the lake today, and some of them have been stealing the bones to take home! The Indian government is now trying to stop this happening, before there are no skeletons left.

▼ Skeleton Lake is located in an uninhabited corner of the Himalayan Mountains.

▲ When the lake melts, skeletons are revealed.

BASHED ON THE HEAD

In 2004, scientists found that the lake contained frozen bodies, along with clothes and jewellery. They dated the victims to the 800s, and found that they all had blows to the head. The latest theory is that the people, en route to a shrine, were wiped out by a storm of giant hailstones!

UNEXPLAINED FACTOR

This one may have been solved, though it's hard to know for sure.

STONEHENGE

Stonehenge, in south-west England, has been baffling visitors for thousands of years. Its one of the world's most famous monuments – but experts still disagree about how it was built, why it is where it is and what it was for.

UNEXPLAINED FACTOR

We've found out a lot about when and how Stonehenge was built. But why? We're still not sure.

? ? ?

MOVING THE STONES

One of the most amazing things about Stonehenge is the size of the stones, which must have been dragged to the site, shaped, stood up on end, and carefully fitted together. Stone age people could do all this, using log rollers, leather ropes and stone tools to shape the stones.

MANY MEANINGS

Stonehenge was built in stages, from around 5000 to 4000 years ago. Bodies have been found there, suggesting it was a burial site – and possibly a temple where people worshipped their ancestors. Its entrance points in the direction of sunrise in midsummer, make some think it was a kind of calendar for working out important dates. Maybe it was all of these!

▼ Stonehenge has several rings of stones. Some of the tallest, called the sarsen stones, have 'lintels' or stone bridges resting on top of them.

GÖBEKLI TEPE

The old and mysterious ancient monument of Göbekli Tepe was only discovered in the 1960s, and excavated and explored in the 1990s. What archaeologists found there completely blew their minds!

▼ Göbeki Tepe is situated at the top of a mountain ridge in the Southeastern Anatolia Region of Turkey.

AMAZINGLY OLD

Göbekli Tepe's stone circles date from 11,000 years ago. That's much older than Stonehenge – it's even much older than Egypt's great pyramids. In fact, 11,000 years ago, most people hadn't even started farming – they mainly survived by hunting and gathering food. Historians used to think these early people couldn't organize complex, artistic construction projects. They were wrong!

UNEXPLAINED FACTOR

So far, this new discovery has created more questions than it's answered!

ANIMAL ART

As they dug, archaeologists found buildings layered on top of each other. The oldest, right at the bottom, are circles of stone pillars, connected by walls. The pillars are T-shaped, up to 6 metres (20 feet) tall, and decorated with carvings. Experts think it could have been a temple where people gathered to worship gods or ancestors. But Göbekli Tepe is still mostly a mystery.

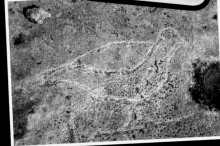

▲ A selection of the carved animal shapes found at Göbekli Tepe.

ATLANTIS

The unexplained legend of Atlantis dates from more than 2000 years ago. Yet people are still fascinated by it, and many think the remains of this ancient, sunken civilization might still be discovered somewhere on the sea floor.

WHAT WAS IT?

The philosopher Plato described Atlantis in around 360 BCE. He said a land of islands, with a great city on a round island in the middle, once lay in the Atlantic Ocean. It was home to an advanced civilization, but their power came to an end when earthquakes and volcanic eruptions sank it beneath the waves.

◀ Could the ancient civilization of Atlantis lie at the bottom of the ocean?

UNEXPLAINED FACTOR

There's no clear explanation so far – unless Plato was making it up!

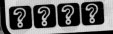

SANTORINI

One theory is that Atlantis was really Santorini, an island in the Mediterranean. It is ring-shaped, with an island in the middle, and was home to the ancient and complex Minoan civilization. Around 1600 BCE, it was devastated by a volcanic eruption which buried the city and also caused a tsunami. The time and place are wrong, but could a garbled version of this event lie behind Plato's story?

WHERE IS IT?

In several parts of the world, underwater ruins have been found. It's rare, but buildings and streets really can get covered by the sea, thanks to changing sea levels, or earthquakes that shift sections of land around. But there's no sign of a city where Atlantis was supposed to be.

YONAGUNI MONUMENT

This underwater structure, lying in the sea near Yonaguni island in Japan, is mind-bogglingly mysterious. Some claim it's a pyramid or boat-dock carved by humans, while others say it could be a natural formation, shaped by the sea. What do you think?

▼ Could this structure have been created by humans – or is it a natural formation?

STEPS, SHAPES AND PLATFORMS

Since being discovered in 1987, the monument has been measured, mapped and photographed. It's about 150 metres (500 feet) long, 40 metres (130 feet) wide and 25 metres (80 feet) tall, and covered in platforms and staircases. There is a star-shaped platform on the top, and a carving on one side that looks like a long face with two hollow eyes.

▲ A drawing of the monument's shape and layout.

LAYERS OF ROCK

The monument is made from sandstone, which can break apart into neatly shaped layers and sections. But the shapes seem so carefully designed, it is hard to believe they formed naturally.

COSTA RICA STONE SPHERES

In the 1930s, a fruit company began clearing forests in Costa Rica in Central America for farming. As they went, they found mysterious stone spheres. Some were tiny – but the biggest were around 2.5 metres (8 feet) across – yet still smooth and spherical.

▶ The spheres are located in the Delta Disquis region of Costa Rica.

WHO MADE THEM?

More than 300 balls have been found, mostly near the remains of pottery and buildings that date from between 600 AD to 1500. This suggests the balls were made by societies that lived here at that time, such as the Diquis people. When invaders from Europe arrived in the 1500s, these cultures died out. So no one knows why the balls were made, or what they were used for. Another mystery is how they made the balls so round. Some have said early peoples with simple tools couldn't have done this, so the spheres must have been made by aliens!

◀ Discovered in the 1930s, some of the spheres date from 600 AD.

PERFECT SPHERES?

At first glance, the spheres look perfect. However, measurements have shown they are not exactly spherical – most are a bit wonky. Some also have scratch marks made by chipping and scraping tools. This points to humans, not aliens, at work!

NAZCA LINES

If you flew over the Nazca Desert in Peru, you would be able to see pictures and patterns cut into the ground by people who lived there around 2000 years ago. They include spirals, geometric shapes and animal figures – a monkey, a spider, a lizard and many more. But what were they for?

UNEXPLAINED FACTOR

The alien theory is quite unlikely! There's probably a more down-to-earth explanation.

? ? ?

◄ The famous Nazca spider. Imagine walking around and around all those legs!

▼ Lines were made by removing the surface layer, revealing a paler clay underneath.

SEEN FROM THE SKY

As it's easiest to see the images from the air, some people have wondered if they were made for ancient gods to look down at – or even to guide alien spaceships to a good landing spot! However, you can see the pictures from nearby hills too, and they could have been mapped out using careful measurements.

LINES FOR WALKING

Another theory is that the shapes were used as pathways for walking along during religious rituals or ceremonies. Each figure is made up of a single line that joins up into a loop, so you can walk all the way around it.

WALLS OF SAKSAYWAMAN

Saksaywaman is a ruined hill fort in Peru, guarded by zigzag-shaped walls built from huge stone boulders. What's most amazing about the walls is that the boulders have been carved and shaped to fit together exactly, with no mortar or cement.

UNEXPLAINED FACTOR

No one knows exactly how they did it!

? ? ? ?

HEAD OF A PUMA

The ancient city of Cuzco is said to be laid out in the shape of a puma (a South American big cat), with Saksaywaman as the head. Its zigzag walls are sometimes called the teeth of the puma.

WHO BUILT IT?

The Inca people used Saksaywaman as a fortress to protect the city of Cuzco. When Spanish invaders arrived in the 1500s, the Inca told them the fort had been there for centuries, and parts of it existed before their time. So the walls might date back as far as the 1100s. It's a mystery how the builders could have shaped and lined up the boulders so accurately, using only simple tools to cut them, and ropes and mounds of earth to haul them up on top of each other.

SOFT STONE?

Some have suggested ancient Peruvians discovered a way to dissolve stone to make a kind of soft clay. That would explain the 'squashed' look of the stones and their close fit. But it's just as likely that the builders were simply brilliant stone carvers.

EASTER ISLAND STATUES

Easter Island, a tiny volcanic island in the eastern Pacific Ocean, is famous for its giant stone statues with massive heads. The carved statues, which are up to 10 metres (30 feet) tall, have short, stocky bodies, but they don't have legs!

KNOCK THEM DOWN!

By the time outsiders discovered Easter Island in 1722, a lot of the island's trees and wildlife had gone, and there was a shortage of food. The clans went to war and pushed down each other's Maoi. Others fell over during earthquakes.

▶ The statues are famous for their big noses, long ears and sharp, jutting chins. Their hollow eyes probably held eyeballs made of coral.

UNEXPLAINED FACTOR

There are still a lot of unanswered questions about the mysterious Maoi.

OURS IS BETTER THAN YOURS!

The statues, known as Maoi, date from around 1200 to 1500, when the Rapa Nui people lived on the island. Archaeologists think they represent ancestors or chiefs, and that different groups competed with each other to build the biggest and best Maoi. What we don't know is how the Rapa Nui moved the statues. They could have been dragged on rolling logs, or 'walked' in an upright position by tilting them from side to side using ropes.

◀ Half-finished Maoi lie in the island's quarry, overgrown with grass.

PYRAMIDS OF GIZA

The Great Pyramid of Giza stands in the Egyptian desert near Cairo. At around 140 metres (460 feet), it was the tallest structure on Earth for nearly 4000 years, from 2560 BCE, when it was completed, until the 1300s, when church spires began to overtake it.

CITY OF DEATH

Ancient Egyptian pharaohs (kings) built the pyramids as tombs for their mummified bodies to lie in when they died. They are part of the Giza Necropolis, or 'death city', which is made up of ancient tombs, temples and graveyards. The pyramids would have required thousands of workers to build them. Experts estimate the Great Pyramid took at least 20 years to construct. To get stones up the sides of the pyramid, they might have used earth ramps or wooden ladders that the stones could be dragged or pushed up.

▼ The largest of the Pyramids of Giza is the Great Pyramid, a tomb for a pharaoh named Khufu.

SMOOTH AND SHINY

In ancient times, the pyramids would have looked even more amazing than they do now. Their stepped slopes were filled in with sections of pale stone to give them smooth, white sides that would have gleamed in the Sun. Most of this casing stone has now come off.

◀ The Great Pyramid still has some of its casing stones near the top.

THE SPHINX

East of Giza's pyramids stands a statue of a sphinx – a creature with a lion's body and a human head and face. It's the biggest statue in the world to have been carved out of a single, solid piece of rock.

WHOSE FACE?

The ancient Egyptians traditionally made sphinx statues with the head of a god or one of their great pharaohs. Experts agree the Sphinx of Giza is probably a likeness of Pharaoh Khafra, whose pyramid lies nearby, and was carved during his reign, from 2558–2532 BCE. However, no one knows why it was put there.

▼ A lot of the soft sandstone the Sphinx is made of has weathered away.

UNEXPLAINED FACTOR

Like its strange, secretive facial expression, the Sphinx is still very mysterious.

❓❓❓❓

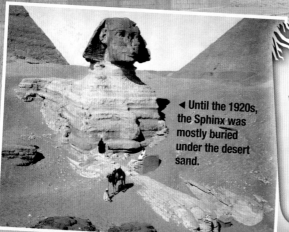

◄ Until the 1920s, the Sphinx was mostly buried under the desert sand.

RIDDLE OF THE SPHINX

In ancient Greek legend, the Sphinx was a monster with a lion's body, a woman's head and birds' wings. She strangled and ate anyone who could not answer her riddle: What has four legs, then two legs, then three legs? Can you answer it?

SAQQARA BIRD

The Saqqara Bird – or Bird Plane – was found in a tomb in Saqqara, Egypt, and is thought to date from about 200 BCE. It's a small wooden model of a flying bird – but it has some features that make it different from most Egyptian bird carvings.

BIRD OR PLANE?

The bird has a long, straight body, and its wings are very unlike a real bird's wings. Instead, they form a flat, wide shape that curves down slightly, just like modern aircraft wings. The bird's tail, instead of being horizontal, is a vertical flap, like a rudder. This has led some people to think the bird could be a model of an aircraft, and even that the Egyptians might have built real flying gliders. Large models of the Saqqara Bird, made from lighter wood and with a flat tailplane added, have been tested in wind tunnels. They flew!

▲ In this picture you can clearly see the bird's plane-like wings.

◄ An outline of the Saqqara Bird's shape as seen from above.

ANCIENT HERCULES

The bird's shape has been compared to modern aircraft, including the Hercules military transport plane. Can you see a similarity?

► A C-130 Hercules in flight.

BAIGONG PIPES

In a remote part of China lies Mount Baigong. The pipe-like features on and around it only became well-known in 2002. According to reports, local people put the pipes down to visits by aliens in ancient times! Could that be true?

CAVES AND LAKES

In one of the caves on Mount Baigong, there are strange pipe-like formations across the ceiling and leading into the floor. More pipes have been found in nearby lakes, and sticking up through the top of the mountain. They are described as looking like ancient, rusty metal – but installing metal pipes inside a mountain seems an unlikely activity for ancient people.

ALIEN LANDING ZONE

The top of Mount Baigong has an odd shape a bit like a pyramid, leading to speculation that aliens came here many centuries ago, and used the mountain as part of a building project.

▼ A section of Baigong pipes.

ARE THEY NATURAL?

It's hard to find out much more about the pipes, as they are in such a remote spot. But some studies have suggested the pipes could be ancient fossilized remains of trees, with deposits of other minerals built up around them. Alternatively, they could be cave formations built up by dripping water. Limestone caves in other parts of the world sometimes have tube-like formations.

ANTIKYTHERA MECHANISM

Did people long ago have more complex technology than we once thought? The Antikythera mechanism shows that they did! Found on a shipwreck near the Greek island of Antikythera around 1900, this ancient machine is a cross between a clock and an early computer.

WORKING IT OUT

The mechanism is thought to date from about 100 BCE, or earlier. At first, no one was sure how it worked. Scientists then discovered it had many gears that fitted together, inscribed with symbols. As the gears moved, they showed the cycles of the Sun and Moon, and predicted when eclipses would occur. It may also have showed the movements of the five planets known to the Ancient Greeks. There's still a lot more to be discovered about what it could do.

▲ The Antikythera shipwreck also contained Greek pottery, statues and coins.

◄ The Antikythera mechanism as it can be seen today, in a museum in Athens.

BAGHDAD BATTERIES

We think of electricity as a modern thing. The earliest batteries invented in Europe date from no earlier than the 1800s. But some people think simple batteries were known in ancient times, in what is now Iraq.

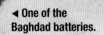
◄ One of the Baghdad batteries.

IT LOOKS LIKE A BATTERY...

The Baghdad batteries were found in the 1930s in Khujut Rabu near Baghdad, and are about 2000 years old. Each one is made up of a clay jar with a lid. Attached to the lid is an iron rod surrounded by a cylinder of copper. The archaeologist who first studied them, Wilhelm König, thought they looked like batteries, and could have been used for electroplating – using an electric current in an acidic liquid to transfer a thin layer of metal onto an object.

BATTERIES
Recent wars in Iraq mean that the Baghdad batteries and other ancient treasures, stored in Baghdad's National Museum of Iraq, have been at risk of damage and looting. Thousands of items have been lost.

UNEXPLAINED FACTOR
The debate on the Baghdad batteries is still going strong!

IT WORKS LIKE A BATTERY...

To test the idea, scientists have made models of the jars, filled them with fruit juice (a weak acid) and wired them up to see if they generated an electric current. They did!

BUT IS IT A BATTERY?

However, that doesn't mean the jars were designed to be batteries – just that they are made of metals that happen to work this way. They could simply be some kind of storage jar, perhaps designed to hold a roll of paper.

OAKVILLE BLOBS

In the summer of 1994, the residents of Oakville, Washington, USA, experienced a strange kind of rain. At first it looked like hailstones, but instead of being hard and icy, they were soft, sticky blobs of gloop.

UNEXPLAINED FACTOR

The case has gone down in mystery history, and is still debated today.

? ? ? ?

GERMS FROM THE SKY?

One police officer described how the blobs smeared all over his windcreeen as he was driving along, and had to be wiped off. On a nearby farm, a woman named Dotty Hearn touched the blobs that fell on her land. Both she and the policeman became ill soon afterwards, and a kitten living on the farm died. Did the blobs contain dangerous germs?

◄ The Oakville blobs were said to look like small, soft and squishy bits of hail.

BLOB TESTING

The strange substance was tested and seemed to contain cells that had come from something living. But what? The mystery has never been solved.

BLOBS ON A PLANE

One theory says the blobs could have simply been toilet waste from a passing plane, minus the blue disinfectant that is usually added (perhaps someone forgot to use it that day!). Others say they could have been sprayed deliberately, but it's not clear why.

STAR JELLY

Strange blobs of jelly falling from the sky have been reported since the 1300s. According to legend, it falls after meteor showers, and somehow comes from the stars. This seems unlikely, so what could it really be?

STAR JELLY THEORIES

• Some experts think star jelly is really slime mould, a strange, living thing a bit like a fungus.
• Some star jelly looks like jellyfish. Could they get sucked up from the sea and fall as rain?
• Some animals eat frogs, but vomit up the slimy parts inside them. Yuck!
• However, when scientists study star jelly, they sometimes find no plant or animal cells in it at all. Maybe it really is an unknown substance that comes from space.

◀ Star jelly was found scattered across Scotland in 2009.

UNEXPLAINED FACTOR

These theories could explain some star jelly, but not all of it....

🅡🅡🅡🅡

THE BLOB

In 1950, police officers in Philadelphia, USA, reported seeing a huge blob of star jelly, 2 metres (6 feet) across, falling to the ground. They tried to pick up the purplish, glowing blob, but it dissolved! A horror film, *The Blob* (1958), was based on this event.

IRVIN S. YEAWORTH, JR.

INDESCRIBABLE...
INDESTRUCTIBLE...
NOTHING CAN STOP IT!

TONY LYN presents
THE BLOB
starring
STEVE McQUEEN
ANETA CORSAUT, STEPHEN CHASE,
EARL ROWE, OLIN HOWLIN,
JOHN BENSON & GEORGE KARAS

◀ *The Blob* starred Steve McQueen.

BALL LIGHTNING

It's likely you've seen lighting, but you probably haven't seen ball lightning. It's a very rare, peculiar kind of lightning that sometimes appears during thunderstorms.

HOW BIG?

Most reports of ball lightning describe it as something about the size of a tennis or cricket ball – but some are smaller, and some much bigger. An example that appeared in a church in Devon, UK, in 1638 was said to be 2.5 metres (8 feet) across!

▶ Ball lightning must have a scientific explanation, but it can be a strange and spooky sight.

UNEXPLAINED FACTOR

It's still very strange and very rare, but we're getting closer to an explanation.

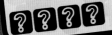

FLOATING AND FIERY

People who have seen ball lightning describe it as a glowing, floating ball of fire or light, which sometimes also makes a hissing or crackling noise. It has been known to bounce off floors or objects, melt its way through glass windows, and burn or even kill people who touch it. Usually, it only lasts for a few seconds before fizzling out, or sometimes exploding with a loud pop or bang.

▲ A scientist named Georg Richmann was killed by ball lightning while doing experiments in a thunderstorm in 1753.

FLYING SAUCER CLOUDS

If you were zooming along in a car and saw this out of the corner of your eye, you could think it was a flying saucer! Look more closely, though, and you can see it's a strangely shaped cloud.

▲ A scarily UFO-like lenticular cloud.

FLYING LENTILS

These clouds are called lenticular clouds (meaning shaped like a lentil), and form near the tops of mountains. Damp wind flows up and continues upwards in a wave until it gets cold enough to condense and form a cloud. The cloud piles up above the mountain, forming layers of disk-like shapes.

AAARRGGH! ALIENS!

Lenticular clouds are often a bit stretched out or lopsided, but occasionally they do look exactly like a flying saucer. As they're rare and not very well-known, they could actually explain some recorded UFO sightings.

MORE WEIRD CLOUDS

Another bizarre cloud formation is the mammatus cloud, which looks like a mass of huge spheres or droplets dangling from a larger cloud.

◄ Mammatus clouds photographed in Canada.

RED RAIN OF KERALA

For two months in the year 2001, Kerala in Southern India was pelted with showers of red rain. Some of it was such a deep red it stained people's clothes pink. The showers began with a loud bang and flash in the sky.

RED RAIN MYSTERY

It sounds scary, but there are actually several reasons why rain can be red. For example, red dust from deserts, or reddish waste chemicals from factories, can blow in the wind and get mixed into rain-clouds. But when the Kerala red rain was examined, it didn't contain either of these things. It contained microscopic oval capsules that looked like spores or cells from something living.

LIFE FROM SPACE?

Some scientists think comets really can carry living cells to Earth from space. Some even say this could be how life actually got started on Earth in the first place!

◄ Heavy downpours of red-coloured rain fell on the southern Indian state of Kerala.

UNEXPLAINED FACTOR

Red rain still falls occasionally in Kerala, and scientists don't agree on what's in it....

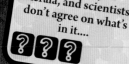

LICHEN OR ALIENS?

One study decided the capsules came from a kind of red lichen that can be found in the area. But another claimed the cells were not from any living things found on Earth, and must have come from space – perhaps from an exploding comet.

ANIMAL RAIN

YOU DROPPED YOUR FISH!

Another possibility is that flocks of birds pick up the fish or frogs, then drop them all at once. But why would they do that!?

Since ancient Greek and Roman times, it has, once in a while, rained animals. Usually, these strange animal showers involve fish or frogs, but tadpole rain, worm rain, crab rain, and even baby alligator rain have also been reported.

◄ Fish pour down from the stormy skies....

UNEXPLAINED FACTOR

Animal rain definitely happens, but we're really not sure how!

❓❓❓❓

▼ An illustration of fish rain dating from 1555.

SUCKED UP?

Most of these creatures have something in common – they are found in water. The main theory for how this happens is that waterspouts (a kind of tornado over water) suck up shoals of fish or other creatures into the air. Then they fall onto the land somewhere nearby. This is the best explanation we have so far – but no one has seen the 'sucking up' happening, and some scientists say waterspouts aren't really strong enough to do this.

45

EARTHQUAKE LIGHTS

If you're ever close to an earthquake as it happens, you might see strange flashes of rainbow light in the sky above, or flickers or balls of light close to the ground. They are known as earthquake lights.

WHAT LIGHTS?

Earthquake lights have been reported for centuries. Some people used to think they were signs from God, and some have mistaken them for UFOs. In fact, up until the 1960s, earthquake scientists didn't believe they really existed – they thought people were imagining them. But once they began to be captured on film, scientists began to take them seriously.

WARNING SIGN!
Earthquakes lights sometimes appear before an earthquake strikes, so they can act as a useful warning!

EARTH LIGHTNING

What causes them? It's now thought earthquake lights are caused by a build-up of electrical charge, a bit like lightning. But instead of coming from the sky, the electricity is generated when some types of rocks are torn apart, and shoots upwards from the ground.

UNEXPLAINED FACTOR

Earthquake lights were a mystery for centuries, but we now know a lot more about them.

? ?

▶ Before the great 1906 San Francisco earthquake, witnesses saw 'streams' of light flowing along the ground.

NAGA FIREBALLS

Every autumn, along the Mekong River in Thailand, people celebrate the religious festival of Wan Ok Phansa. Around this time, it's said that you can see burning balls of light rising up out of the river, and shooting into the sky.

UNEXPLAINED FACTOR

There are a lot of arguments about the fireballs. You might have to go and check them out for yourself!

? ? ? ?

DO THEY EXIST?

It's hard to say if the fireballs are real, as the festival also features fireworks and guns being fired. Some think the lights that can be seen shooting into the sky are really tracer rounds – bullets that light up as they fly through the air. Others say that at this time of year, gas that has collected at the bottom of the river bubbles up to the surface, and catches fire when it mixes with oxygen. This can happen, especially in marshy areas. Maybe the display is a mixture of natural and artificial lights.

◀ In Thailand, the Naga is said to spit fire into the sky.

BURPS OF THE NAGA

Local legend tells of a mythical water dragon, the Naga, that lives deep in the river. The fireballs are said to be bubbles of its fiery breath.

PAULDING LIGHT

Near Paulding, Michigan, USA, a strange, flickering light appears at night. If you stand in the right place, you can see it between the trees. The Paulding light – also called the Dog Meadow Light – is almost always there.

SPOOKY STORIES

The light first began to appear in the 1960s, and ghostly legends have risen up around it. Some say a railway worker was crushed between two train carriages, and his ghost still carries a lantern around the valley. Another tale claims the light is the ghost of a murdered train driver.

TRAFFIC LIGHTS

In 2010, some students used a telescope to look at the Paulding light closely. They decided it was caused by car headlights on a distant road, reflected and channelled by a kind of mirage effect that makes them visible from the viewing point.

▲ The Paulding light as it appears every night.

UNEXPLAINED FACTOR

Car headlights make a convincing explanation – though some are still sure the light is supernatural!

GLOWING GASES?

In some places, gas that catches alight does rise out of the ground. This is another possible explanation for the Paulding light, but it would be unlikely to last for so many years.

CROP CIRCLES

In the 1970s, patterns began appearing in fields in England. The stalks of the crops had been bent to the ground, creating groups of circles or other shapes. The circles caused a sensation – where had they come from?

LOTS OF THEORIES

Some people thought the circles must have been formed by a kind of ancient energy inside the Earth. Others said aliens had put them there as a message to humans. Some scientists thought they could have been formed by windstorms.

IT WAS US!

In 1991, two British men, Doug Bower and Dave Chorley, revealed they had started the phenomenon by making the circles themselves, using ropes and planks to measure out the shapes and flatten the crops.

COMMERCIAL CIRCLES

Today, companies pay crop circle makers to create advertising slogans or logos in crop circle form.

◄ The logo of the Mitsubishi company in a field of wheat.

OUT-OF-BODY EXPERIENCES

At least one in 10 people have experienced the feeling of being 'outside' their own bodies. It is most likely to happen as you're falling asleep, if you faint, or if you're under a general anaesthetic to have surgery. But can you really leave your body, or is it just an illusion?

SEEING YOURSELF

Many people who report having out-of-body experiences, or OBEs, say they could see themselves lying in bed or on the operating table. But scientists think this isn't real – it's more like a vivid dream, created by your imagination, not anything you can really 'see'. After all, your eyes are still in your body!

UNEXPLAINED FACTOR

OBEs are still not understood, and scientists do lots of experiments on them.

❓❓❓❓

◄ An OBE feels as if you are floating away from your own body.

▼ Patients have experienced OBEs when under general anaesthetic.

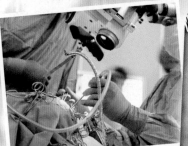

OPERATION OBE

An American woman, Pamela Reynolds, had a well-known OBE in 1991 in which she saw her own brain operation, and the tools that were used. Experts still debate whether this was proof of a 'real' OBE.

SLIDERS

Sliders are people who claim that when they go near electrical appliances, they make them go wrong. (The name sliders comes from the phrase 'Street Light Interference', or SLI.) Typically, sliders report that street lights flicker or go out as they walk under them.

UNEXPLAINED FACTOR

SLI is still mysterious and unproved – but that could change.

RANDOM CHANCE

Remember, electric devices go wrong and light bulbs burn out all the time, so if it happens near you once or twice, it's not strange at all. But if it happens ALL THE TIME – maybe you're a slider!

COUD IT BE TRUE?

Our brains do work using electrical signals, so it's possible that some people have extra-strong electrical brainwaves that interfere with technology. People who claim to be sliders often say the effect is worse when they are stressed, angry, or thinking hard.

▶ Being a slider could be frustrating if it makes your gadgets go wrong.

PSYCHOKINESIS

Psychokinesis means 'mind-movement'. It's also known as telekinesis, or 'distance-movement'. Basically, it means being able to make things move using the power of your mind.

MOVING OBJECTS

In the early 1900s, Stanislawa Tomczyk from Poland was photographed making objects levitate. In the 1960s, films showed Nina Kulagina from Russia moving matches and small boxes on a table in front of her without touching them.

◄ Polish medium Stanislawa Tomczyk levitates a pair of scissors while in a trance.

WHY ISN'T IT EASIER?

If psychokinesis does exist, it must be very rare and hard to do. As some scientists have pointed out, if it was real, it should be easy to measure, and more of us would be doing it.

UNEXPLAINED FACTOR

Attempts to prove psychokinesis exists have not got very far.

HANG ON A MINUTE!

These sound impressive, but if you think about it, they could be exaggerated claims, and the films and photos – which are very old and blurry – could be faked using hidden magnets or strings. Modern scientists have tried to test psychokinesis properly in the laboratory, and they have found no clear, solid evidence for it.

TELEPATHY

Telepathy is the ability to send messages to someone else using just your mind. It often features in sci-fi films, but is it real?

I KNEW IT WAS YOU!

Many people think they've experienced telepathy. The most common example is when the phone rings, and before answering it, you 'just know' who is calling. Other examples of telepathy involve suddenly worrying about someone, only to find that at that moment they were in danger.

TELEPATHY TESTS

However, like many other mysterious phenomena, strict scientific tests for telepathy don't seem to prove much – just a very slight effect in some experiments. This could be because telepathy only happens occasionally, or is affected by strong emotions, which are hard to create in a lab.

DO YOUR OWN TEST!

To test for telepathy, scientists use cards with symbols on them. One person chooses a card and tries to 'send' the symbol on it to another person, who sits somewhere else out of sight, using their mind. The 'receiver' has to draw the picture they think is being sent.

▲ Zenner cards are often used in telepathy experiments.

ESP

ESP, or Extra-Sensory Perception, is being aware of things without using your senses. Telepathy is one type of ESP, but it also means being able to see the future, sense where a hidden object is, or even 'see' inside a building that you are nowhere near.

SEEING THINGS

Some people claim to have seen accidents in their minds just before they happened. But this could be just a coincidence. If something you have just thought about then happens, you are more likely to notice and remember it.

REMOTE VIEWING

Sensing unseen or distant objects is known as remote viewing. The US government worked with remote viewers to see if they could work as spies.

WRECK OF THE TITAN(IC)

In 1898, Morgan Robertson wrote a story about a ship called the *Titan* that hit an iceberg and sank. Fourteen years later his story 'came true' when the real-life *Titanic* sank. Did he see into the future, or was it coincidence?

SPONTANEOUS HUMAN COMBUSTION

In a typical case of spontaneous human combustion (SHC), someone burns to death in their home. Sometimes there's just a heap of ashes left – along with the person's feet, which are often undamaged. Weird!

DON'T PANIC!

The term 'spontaneous human combustion' does mean bursting into flames with no good reason. But don't worry – it's unlikely to happen to you! Most of the victims on record were old or unwell in some way, making it hard for them to move around. They were usually heavy smokers too. Experts think that rather than suddenly exploding, they were set alight by a cigarette or a spark from an open fire, and then burned very slowly, a bit like a candle.

◄ An alarming case of spontaneous combustion!

LEGS LEFT BEHIND

Why are victims' legs and feet often unburned? Scientists think this is simply because flames burn upwards. If someone is sitting in a chair, their body could burn, while their legs, pointing down, escape the flames.

◄ The scene after a famous case of SHC, the death of Dr John Bentley in 1966.

BORLEY RECTORY

Borley Rectory was renowned as one of the most haunted houses in Britain. It was destroyed by fire in 1939, and the ruins were pulled down in 1944. But until then, families living in the rectory, and visitors to it, reported hearing strange noises, and seeing ghosts.

▲ Borley Rectory in its haunted heyday.

HARRY PRICE

In 1929, the haunted rectory made the national news, and ghost hunter Harry Price went to investigate. He said the haunting was real and wrote a famous book about it. But some people think he might have created some of the ghostly activity himself!

THE PHANTOM NUN

According to legend, a monastery stood on the site in medieval times. One of the monks had fallen in love with a local nun, and they planned to run away together. But they were caught and sentenced to death. Gruesomely, the nun was bricked up alive inside a wall in the rectory. Her ghost was seen wandering around the rectory, or looking in at the windows.

However, after the rectory was no more, several people who had been there said they thought many of the spooky goings-on were faked, to make money from newspapers and visitors.

THE BROWN LADY OF RAYNHAM HALL

The picture on this page is one of the most famous ghost photos ever taken. It's said to show a ghost called the Brown Lady, as she appears in her favourite spot, the staircase of Raynham Hall in Norfolk, England.

WHO WAS SHE?

The Brown Lady is said to be Dorothy Walpole, who died in the house in 1726. Her husband Charles Townshend is believed to have locked her indoors after he found out she had had an affair. Since then, many visitors have reported seeing her, wearing a brown dress, gliding down the stairs or appearing in hallways and bedrooms (sometimes with her eyes missing!).

THE PHOTO

Two magazine photographers snapped the strange, glowing figure on a visit to Raynham Hall in 1936. Though the photograph doesn't look faked, it's possible the shape was made by light leaking into the camera somehow. What do you think?

▲ The famous photo of the Brown Lady.

UNEXPLAINED FACTOR

Even if the photo is a fake, this well-documented ghost is hard to explain away!

**??? **

HEADING HERE

One witness, Frederick Maryatt, was so scared by seeing the Brown Lady (who, he claimed, gave him a scary grin!) that he shot his gun at her. He said the bullet went straight through her, and got stuck in a wall.

MYRTLES PLANTATION

Myrtles Plantation in Louisiana is famous for being one of the most haunted houses in the USA. And if you'd like to try to spot its ghosts, you can actually go and stay overnight there, as it's now a guest house!

IN THE MIRROR

Some visitors believe the ghosts are trapped in a haunted mirror, and look to see if they can spot them.

▲ The Myrtles Plantation.

◄ Has this photo captured the ghost of Chloe hiding behind a pillar? Or is it just a shadow?

UNEXPLAINED FACTOR

It may not be as spooky as it seems, but where these legends came from is a mystery.

HOW MANY GHOSTS?

At least 10 ghosts are reported to roam the house. The best-known is the ghost of a slave girl named Chloe, who is said to have worked there in the 1820s. According to legend, she accidentally killed the plantation owner's family with a cake containing deadly poison – so they all haunt the house as well! Another scary ghost is William Winter, who was shot at the house in 1871 and died after crawling up the stairs – where some say he can still be seen....

ROSE HALL

According to legend, haunted Rose Hall in Jamaica is the site of as series of unimaginably horrible happenings – including murders and scary magic curses. But how terrifying is it really?

THE WHITE WITCH

The story says that in the 1820s, an English woman named Annie Palmer was the mistress of the house, and ruled her slaves and servants mercilessly. If any of them annoyed her, she had them killed or cast terrible curses on them. Finally, she was killed herself when her angry slaves turned against her. She gained the nickname 'The White Witch of Rose Hall' and is said to haunt the mansion to this day.

ROMANTIC ROSE HALL

Rose Hall fell into ruins, but was restored in the 1960s. Now the beautiful house and gardens are home to a museum and restaurant, and is a popular venue for weddings!

▲ This tomb in the grounds of Rose Hall is known as Annie Palmer's grave, but the real Annie was buried somewhere else. Also, although Annie did exist, there's no evidence she was the scary witch of legend!

▼ Rose Hall, Jamaica.

THE STANLEY HOTEL

Every year, people visit the Stanley Hotel in Colorado, USA, to spot ghosts. The hotel is famous for inspiring writer Stephen King to write his scary novel *The Shining*, which was later turned into an even scarier film.

▼ The Stanley Hotel is famed for its beautiful views.

UNEXPLAINED FACTOR

As the ghost stories help the hotel's business, it's hard to say how genuine they are.

HAPPY GHOSTS

Real-life reports of ghosts aren't always frightening. Ghosts sometimes seem to happily go about their business without upsetting anyone, like the Stanley Hotel ghosts.

▲ The Stanley Hotel ballroom.

ROOM 217

Stephen King wrote his book after he stayed in room 217. It's said that in 1911, a maid was seriously hurt in this room by a gas explosion. After her death, she came back to haunt to room – but in a nice way! She unpacks people's bags and moves things around. Some say that this happened to Stephen King during his stay.

GHOSTLY PARTIES

According to staff and guests, other happenings include hearing the sounds of a party in the empty ballroom, and children laughing and playing upstairs, especially in room 418 – even when there are no children around. Flora Stanley, the wife of the man who built the hotel, haunts the downstairs areas and sometimes plays the piano.

WINCHESTER MYSTERY HOUSE

The Winchester Mystery House near San Jose in California, USA, has staircases that lead straight into the ceiling, sealed-off rooms and doors that open halfway up the side of the house. But why?

▲ Winchester Mystery House, San Jose, California, USA.

SARAH WINCHESTER

The house was built by Sarah Winchester, a wealthy widow whose husband had made a fortune from the Winchester gun company. Work on the house went on from 1884 until Sarah died in 1922. As she was rich, she could keep a team of builders on site all the time. The story goes that Sarah did this because she thought she was being haunted by all the people who had been killed by Winchester guns. She was said to go to a special room every night to meet the spirits and receive building instructions. She constantly rebuilt and rearranged rooms to keep the ghosts happy.

VISIT THE MYSTERY HOUSE!

Today the house is a museum that holds guided ghost-hunting tours, including some at night.

▲ Some doors and stairways lead to nowhere.

ABRAHAM LINCOLN

The White House, the residence of US presidents, is one of the most famous haunted houses. It's best-known ghost is former president Abraham Lincoln who was president during America's Civil War of 1861 to 1865.

POLITE GHOST

Like other presidents, Lincoln lived and worked in the White House, and many people, including staff, guests and even other presidents, claim to have seen or heard him. The ghost is heard walking up corridors, and knocking at bedroom doors. In 1941, when the Queen of the Netherlands was visiting, she said she heard a knock at the door, opened it, and saw Lincoln standing there! Others have seen him sitting in chairs or on a bed, taking his boots off.

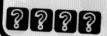

UNEXPLAINED FACTOR

One of the world's best-documented and frequently seen ghosts.

? ? ? ?

▼ Lincoln was shot while at a performance at Ford's Theatre in Washington DC. He died on 15 April 1865.

LINCOLN'S DREAM

Lincoln himself is said to have had a spooky experience in the White House. Shortly before his death, he dreamed he was walking through the White House and came across his own funeral. When he asked, he was told the president had been assassinated. Not long after, Lincoln was assassinated, while going to the theatre in April 1865.

THE FLYING DUTCHMAN

Ghosts aren't just people – they can also be animals or objects. The Flying Dutchman is a famous ghost sailing ship, said to roam the seas forever, bringing doom and disaster to anyone who sees it.

◀ The ghostly ship appears through the mist....

SPOOKY SIGHTINGS

Many sailors have sworn they've seen the ghostly Dutchman, sailing through the air, or coming towards their ship then vanishing at the last moment. One was a British prince who later became King George V. He described the Flying Dutchman as, "a strange red light as of a phantom ship all aglow".

SHIPS IN THE AIR

What witnesses probably saw was a mirage. This happens when layers of warm and cool air bend light, making a ship that is far away below the horizon appear as a faint image in the air above it.

LEGEND OF THE DUTCHMAN

Most stories say that the ghost ship was a merchant ship or warship sailing past the Cape of Good Hope, at the Southern tip of Africa in the 1600s. A storm blew up, but the captain was determined to make his way around the Cape. But the ship sank, and its ghost must keep sailing forever!

UNEXPLAINED FACTOR

Spooky stories surround the Flying Dutchman, but it can be explained as a mirage.

THEATRE ROYAL GHOST

The Theatre Royal, Drury Lane, is a famous old theatre in London, UK, that's said to be home to a host of ghosts.

THE MAN IN GREY

Most often seen is a ghost known as the Man in Grey. This ghost always appears in an 18th-century outfit with a three-cornered hat, a powdered wig and a grey cape. He sits in a seat in the Upper Circle, then walks along the row of seats and through a wall. Spotting him while rehearsing is said to be good luck for the show!

Other spooks at the Theatre Royal include:

• Joseph Grimaldi, a clown from the 1800s.

• Victorian pantomime dame Dan Leno, whose perfume wafts around.

• Charles Macklin, who killed a fellow actor in an argument in 1735.

▼ Since 1663, the Theatre Royal Drury Lane has provided entertainment for the masses.

GHOST RECORDINGS?

Ghosts like the Man in Grey are called 'recording ghosts' because they are reported to appear over and over again, doing the same thing in the same place, like a video recording. This type of ghost supports the idea that ghost sightings could have some kind of scientific explanation.

TOWER OF LONDON GHOSTS

It's no surprise that the 1000-year-old Tower of London has a spooky atmosphere. England's rulers, such as bloodthirsty King Henry VIII, used to send their enemies there to be locked up, or have their heads chopped off!

GHOST OF A BEAR

Animal ghosts are quite rare, but in 1816, a guard at the Tower swore he had seen a ghost bear approaching him! He thought it was real and tried to stab it, but it went right through him. The guard died a few days later.

MEET THE GHOSTS

Ghosts in the Tower include...

▼ The keep, the central part of the Tower of London.

• Henry VIII's wife Anne Boleyn, who was beheaded here, is reported to wander around without her head, sometimes carrying it under her arm!

• The Princes in the Tower – two boys who were locked up in the Tower, and possibly killed, by their uncle, King Richard III, to allow him to grab the throne. People claim to hear their voices all around the Tower.

• Arbella Staurt, who was kept prisoner in part of the Tower called the Queen's House. Her ghost is said to try to strangle people or give them a big shove from behind.

UNEXPLAINED FACTOR

There are a LOT of ghost sightings here, and some of them are quite convincing!

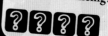

GLAMIS CASTLE

"Hail to thee, Thane of Glamis!" say the three witches in Shakespeare's spooky Scottish play, *Macbeth.* In real life, Macbeth didn't live in Glamis Castle, but plenty of other people lived and died there – some in horribly scary circumstances.

SECRET ROOMS

The castle seems to have several rooms that are bricked off. One is said to contain skeletons of the Ogilvie family, who asked the Lord of Glamis for protection. Instead he walled them up and left them to die – and to haunt the castle! Another story tells of a room where 'Earl Beardie' plays cards for all eternity.

UNEXPLAINED FACTOR

Glamis has a scary history, but many of its stories sound more like myths.

▼ Towering Glamis Castle has a very spooky atmosphere.

TOWEL TEST

According to local legend, a group of visitors to the castle decided to test for secret rooms by hanging towels out of every window they could find. When they looked from the outside, several windows still had no towels!

LADY JANET

In the 1500s, Lady Janet Douglas, the wife of a later Lord of Glamis, was accused of witchcraft and of killing her husband, and burned alive – but the accusations were false. Her ghost, known as Lady Janet or the Grey Lady, is reported to haunt the castle's chapel, and a seat there is traditionally left empty for her.

BALLYGALLY CASTLE

Four-hundred-year-old Ballygally Castle, on the coast of Northern Ireland, is now a hotel. But one of the rooms is never used for guests. It's kept empty for the castle's resident ghost, Lady Isobella Shaw.

LOCKED AWAY

A Scottish Lord, James Shaw, built the castle in the early 1600s, and lived there with his wife, Lady Isobella. But all he wanted from her was an heir. Once she had a baby, he locked her away – possibly in the turret room that is now the 'ghost room'. She tried to escape, but fell from the window and died.

▼ The older part of the castle, with its turret rooms.

UNEXPLAINED FACTOR

The hotel owner and many visitors are convinced something supernatural is going on...

❓❓❓

FRIENDLY GHOST

Sometimes guests sense a strange presence, or hear voices. Some have even said Isobella appeared in their rooms and woke them up, then disappeared. But the ghost is said to be friendly, not frightening.

SMELLY GHOST

Lady Isobella is believed to waft a strange smell, a bit like vanilla, around the hotel. Many reported ghosts are associated with smells, but no one knows why this should be.

EDINBURGH VAULTS

The South Bridge in Edinburgh, Scotland, was completed in 1788. The archways under the bridge had a network of underground rooms and passageways – now called the Edinburgh Vaults. At first, shops used them as storage rooms. Later, families lived there – and crime, even murder, became common.

GHOSTS AND VOICES

Ghosts include a boy called Jack who is said to pinch people and tug at their clothes, and a man called Mr Boots who tells visitors to get out! On at least two occasions, people making TV and radio recordings have found extra voices on them that no one heard at the time.

▲ Villainy was common in the dark, damp Edinburgh Vaults.

BURKE AND HARE

In 1820s Edinburgh, Burke and Hare killed people and sold their bodies for use in medical science. They are thought to have stalked the vaults looking for victims.

KNIGHTON GORGES MANOR

Knighton Gorges Manor on the Isle of Wight, UK, no longer exists – just the gateposts and outbuildings are standing. But the house itself is believed to reappear every New Year's Eve, with a party going on inside!

THE KNIGHTON GORGES CURSE

One of the house's first owners was Hugh de Morville, one of four men who killed the Archbishop of Canterbury, Thomas Becket, in 1170. Hugh fled to Knighton Gorges after the murder, and considered the house cursed from that day on. Various ghosts are now said to haunt the area, including a man on horseback, and a phantom carriage.

▼ Knighton Gorges Manor is said to reappear each New Year's Eve.

GATE GARGOYLES

The spooky gateposts play a part in the haunting. Scary gargoyles (monster statues) are said to sometimes appear on top of them.

KNOCK IT DOWN!

The house met its end in 1821 when the owner at the time, George Bissett, was furious with his daughter for marrying a man he didn't approve of. Bissett had the whole manor torn down out of spite, so that she couldn't inherit it!

FACES OF BELMEZ

In 1971, Maria Gomez Camara discovered a staring face on her concrete kitchen floor. It couldn't be cleaned off, so the face was dug out and new concrete put down... but the face reappeared!

FLOOR FULL OF FACES

Gradually, more faces appeared, in various sizes, some with shoulders and arms. They would change over time, disappear and reappear. Several paranormal experts declared they were a genuine unexplained phenomenon – possibly caused by ghosts from an old graveyard under the house, or mysteriously created by Maria's thoughts.

◀ One of the famous faces of Belmez.

DELAYED EFFECT

Sceptics have suggested that if some kind of acid was used to paint the faces, it would have been invisible at first, only appearing gradually as the concrete reacted with it. This could explain the faces' 'magical' appearance.

UNEXPLAINED FACTOR

Though many people are still convinced, the faces could have been faked – the most likely explanation.

EXPERT TESTING

Some of the faces were cut out and taken away to be tested. Substances such as soot and vinegar were found in the marks, but believers pointed out they could be on a kitchen floor anyway!

FACES OF SS WATERTOWN

When SS Watertown was sailing in the Pacific in 1924, two of the crew died cleaning out a tank. They were buried at sea. Afterwards, other sailors claimed they could see the men's faces in waves alongside the ship.

FAMOUS PHOTO

When the captain reported the watery ghost sighting, his bosses told him to take a camera on the ship's next voyage and see if he could photograph the faces. The picture below was the result.

SUSPICIOUS ARROWS

The photo that appeared in the press had two white arrows added to it to point out the faces. Could they have been used to help cover up signs of tampering?

▼ It's easy to spot the two faces, so did this photo really need such big arrows?

IS IT REAL?

For a long time, this was considered one of the most convincing and unexplained of all ghost photos. More recently, though, several ghost hunters have said they think it was faked. If you look at the photograph closely, the face on the left has a very hard edge. The faces are also very similar and at similar angles, suggesting one might be a copy of the other.

UNEXPLAINED FACTOR

A great example of a scary photo, but it can probably be explained as a hoax.

AMELIA EARHART

In the 1930s, Amelia Earhart was a famous pilot. She had set several world records, including being the first female pilot to fly solo across the Atlantic. But during her biggest challenge, an attempt to fly around the world in 1937, she vanished.

▲ Amelia Earhart in her Lockheed Vega plane flying over Burbank, California in 1934.

NEARLY THERE

In July 1937, Earhart took off with her navigator, Fred Noonan, from New Guinea in southeast Asia, heading across the Pacific to Oakland, California. She planned to stop at Howland Island – but never made it. Due to mixed-up radio messages from nearby ships, Earhart lost her way. There was no sign of the plane, so it was assumed it had run out of fuel and ditched into the sea, sinking and killing both on board. But had it?

UNEXPLAINED FACTOR

This mystery is still unsolved, and the evidence is still being debated.

NEW DISCOVERIES

In the 1980s and 90s, discoveries on Gardner Island, to the south of Howland, suggested the plane might have landed there. They included tools made out of what looked like plane parts, and old records describing how a skeleton matching Amelia Earhart's size and height had been discovered there in 1940. Could she have survived a crash and lived there as a castaway?

▲ Amelia Earheart seated in her plane.

FLIGHT 19

This disappearance in December 1945 involved six aircraft on two missions. The case led to many theories, such as an alien abduction, or giant magnets under the sea, especially as it happened in the Bermuda Triangle (see page 20). But is there a simpler explanation?

TRAINING FLIGHT

Flight 19 was a US Navy training mission, made up of five Avenger planes with 14 crew, led by flight instructor, Charles Taylor. They set off from Fort Lauderdale, Florida, in clear weather at around 2.30 pm. A few hours later, they had all vanished. A last message from Taylor, included the words, "we'll have to ditch unless landfall... we all go down together."

WRONG WAY!

Radio messages earlier in the flight showed Taylor was confused about their location, and may have attempted to head back to base – ending up meeting a storm over the Atlantic and running out of fuel. But why did the seaplane explode? Could it have just been a coincidence?

▼ The crew of the infamous lost flight 19.

UNEXPLAINED FACTOR

No one knowns exactly what did happen – but it probably wasn't aliens.

RESCUE DISASTER

The Navy immediately sent Mariner seaplanes to search for survivors. One plane, with 13 crew on board, also disappeared. A ship in the area reported seeing an explosion, and finding fuel on the sea surface, but no survivors. No one from either flight was ever seen again.

MARY CELESTE

The Mary Celeste set sail from New York in 1872, heading to Italy with a cargo of alcohol. But a month later, she was found drifting, with no one on board. The crew's belongings, food and water were still there, and so was the cargo. Where had they gone?

ROPE CLUE

The sailors who discovered the abandoned Mary Celeste found the lifeboat was missing. There was also a rope tied to the back of the ship. For some reason, it seemed the crew had got into the lifeboat, perhaps tying it to the back of the ship. If it had come undone, they would have been left to starve or sink in the stormy Atlantic.

◄ The Mary Celeste was found in the Atlantic with no one on board.

UNEXPLAINED FACTOR

It's still a mystery, but a sensible explanation could exist.

? ? ?

WHO WAS ON BOARD?

The ship had 10 people on board when it disappeared – Captain Benjamin Briggs, his wife Sarah and two-year-old daughter Sophia, and seven crewmen. None of them were ever seen or heard from again.

ALCOHOL EXPLOSION

The mystery has never been solved, and theories about what happened include all kinds of paranormal possibilities. But a more rational idea is that fumes from the cargo of alcohol leaked out of the hold, or even caused an explosion, leading those on board to take refuge in the lifeboat.

EILEAN MÒR MYSTERY

The Flannan Isles are a group of islands off the northern coast of Scotland. The biggest, Eilean Mòr, is home to a lighthouse. It was here, in December 1900, that the three lighthouse-keepers, the island's sole inhabitants, mysteriously vanished.

THERE'S NO ONE HERE!

On 27 December 1900, after a few stormy weeks, a relief boat arrived to bring supplies and to allow the lighthouse keepers to change shifts. But when the replacement keeper went ashore, he found the lighthouse empty. The doors were shut, and the lamps and kitchen equipment were clean and tidy, but the oilskins were missing, apart from one set, and a chair had been left lying on its side. What happened? While some say ghosts or even alien abduction were to blame, others think all three men could have been swept away by a giant wave.

UNEXPLAINED FACTOR

An unexplained disappearance that will probably never be solved.

◀ Eilean Mòr as it is today. The lighthouse is now automatic and has no crew.

DISAPPEARANCE DATE

The last entry in the lighthouse-keepers' log was early on 15 December, when they reported storm damage to the island. Later that day, a ship sailing past the island had noticed the lighthouse's lamp was out. This must have been the day of the disaster!

PHINEAS GAGE

If an iron bar shot into your face, up through your brain, and out of the top of your head, you would not expect to survive. But Phineas Gage did!

THE ACCIDENT

Gage's job was clearing routes for railways by blasting away rocks. In 1848, he was at work in Vermont, USA, filling a hole with explosives, pressing them down with his iron bar, ready to be ignited. But the bar scraped the rock, making a spark, and the explosion went off early – forcing the iron bar straight through his head!

◀ After the accident, Gage kept the iron bar as a memento. Apart from losing an eye, his face healed up very well.

MISSING BRAINS

Gage lost quite a lot of his brain. Some was found on the iron bar, and a bit more, according to his doctor, fell out while he was vomiting later that day. Ewww!

AMAZING RECOVERY

Instead of dying, Gage went to see a doctor, saying he hoped to be back at work soon. The doctor cleaned and bandaged his wounds, and gradually Gage got better. However, friends reported that his personality changed – from being reliable to being rude and unpredictable – though this later improved. In fact, Gage's case taught experts a lot about how the brain works.

UNEXPLAINED FACTOR

Don't try this at home! Gage's accident really should have killed him.

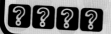

FABRICE MUAMBA

In March 2012, in a match between Tottenham Hotspur and his team Bolton Wanderers, Fabrice Muamba collapsed on the pitch after a heart attack. The first aid team, and a heart doctor who had been watching the game, tried to revive him.

UNEXPLAINED FACTOR

The expert medical help Muamba received saved his life, but doesn't explain how he avoided brain damage.

DEAD FOR 78 MINUTES

Muamba was rushed to hospital and doctors kept trying to restart his heart. After many electric shock treatments, it began working – 78 minutes after it stopped! Without his heart beating, Muamba's brain would have suffered a dangerous shortage of oxygen. If he lived, there was a risk of serious brain-damage.

▲ Doctors battle to save Muamba on the pitch.

► Fabrice Muamba.

MIRACLE SURVIVAL

Two days later Muamba was awake, and told the doctor his name and that he was a footballer. Though he can no longer play football, and has a special implant to restart his heart if necessary, Muamba has made a full recovery and has started a new career as a sports journalist.

GET WELL SOON!

While Muamba was recovering, his Bolton team-mates all played wearing shirts with his name on, along with get well messages.

VESNA VULOVIC

In 1972, flight attendant Vesna Vulovic was flying over Czechoslovakia (now the Czech Republic) when her plane blew up and broke apart. All the passengers and crew were killed – except Vesna.

SOLE SURVIVOR

Vulovic was found inside the plane, with a serving trolley wedging her in place. She spent nearly a month in hospital in a coma, but made a good recovery. In 1985, she was entered into the Guinness Book of Records for surviving the highest fall with no parachute – an estimated 10,160 metres (33,330 feet)!

UNEXPLAINED FACTOR

Even if she fell from lower than originally thought, Vulovic's survival is incredible.

? ? ? ?

◄ Vesna recovering in hospital after the crash.

LUCKY VESNA

Though Vesna Vulovic herself said there was nothing lucky about the crash (as the 27 other people on board died), "Vesna" became a popular girls' name locally, as people thought it must bring good luck.

OR WAS IT?

In 2009, it was claimed the plane had descended to a low altitude because of technical problems, perhaps looking for a place to land. Flying low over Czechoslovakia, it had been mistaken for an enemy aircraft and and been shot down. However, there's little evidence for this, and no one can be sure.

JULIANE KOEPCKE

Juliane Koepcke not only survived falling from an exploding plane; she also made a nine-day trek through the rainforest to reach safety. She only made it thanks to her determination and survival knowledge.

▲ Juliane Koepcke flew again when she returned to Germany in 1972.

UNEXPLAINED FACTOR

A row of plane seats protected Juliane, and vegetation broke her fall – but her survival is still extraordinary.

? ?

▼ The Peruvian rainforest.

RAINFOREST THUNDERSTORM

In 1971, Juliane Koepcke was 17 and living in Peru, where her German parents worked as biologists. She and her mother, bird expert Maria Koepcke, took a flight to meet Juliane's father in another part of Peru. But 3000 metres (10,000 feet) up in the air, the plane flew into a heavy thunderstorm and was struck by lightning. It disintegrated and plummeted to the ground. Juliane woke up to find herself deep in the jungle, still strapped into her row of three seats. After collecting sweets from the wreckage, she found a river and headed downstream, as she knew this would lead to a village or town. Nine days later, she found a boat shed, where she was eventually rescued.

MAGGOT INFECTION!

On her nine-day river trek, Koepcke was badly bitten by flies and ended up with maggots infecting her arm. As soon as she reached the boatshed, she used some petrol to kill the maggots – a survival tip learnt from her father.

HARRISON OKENE

In May 2013, off the coast of Nigeria, a tugboat capsized and sank in a storm. It was five o'clock in the morning, and most of the crew were asleep in their cabins. Only the cook, Harrison Okene, was up – he had just gone to the bathroom.

TRAPPED!

As the boat sank to the seabed 30 metres (100 feet) down, water flooded the cabins, and Okene became trapped in an air pocket inside the bathroom. He had nothing to drink but a small bottle of cola. Divers reached the boat two and a half days later looking for bodies. When Okene saw a diver's lights shining in the water, he swam to find him. The diver jumped when what he thought was a dead body reached out and grabbed him!

▲ Harrison Okene.

◄ A similar tugboat to the one Okene became trapped in.

UNEXPLAINED FACTOR

Okene's survival can be explained scientifically, but he was also incredibly lucky to be rescued.

60 HOURS OF AIR

Okene only had a small amount of air to breathe, and normally the oxygen in it would only have lasted a few hours. So how did he survive? Experts think that as the boat sank, the water pressure squeezed a larger amount of the air into a smaller space – so it contained a higher concentration of oxygen than normal air.

PAUL TEMPLER

Bolts through the brain, air crashes, sunken ships – these things are pretty hard to survive. But what about being SWALLOWED BY A HIPPOPOTAMUS!? How one man managed to escape from that is a truly amazing story — especially as most human-hippo encounters do NOT end well.

HIPPO ATTACK

In 1996, Paul Templer worked as a wildlife guide on the Zambezi river in Africa. He was leading a group of canoes down river, when a hippo came up underneath one of the boats and tipped its guide out. Templer paddled over to try to rescue the guide, but just as he did so, everything went dark.

◄ Hippos are among Africa's deadliest animals.

UNEXPLAINED FACTOR

If you get this close to a hippo, you're normally toast. Templer's survival was a one-in-a-million.

? ? ?

DEADLY HIPPOS

You may think of hippos as slow, peaceful creatures, but they kill hundreds of people every year. They have huge, razor-sharp tusks, and are quick to attack if they think anyone is invading their stretch of river.

SLIMY BUT NOT WET!

Templer recalled being somewhere dark and smelly, then realised he was halfway down the hippo's throat! The hippo spat him out, but struck again, biting Templer and dragging him deep under the water. However, he got away and finally made it to hospital. He lost an arm, but survived. Sadly, another guide did not.

LUBBOCK LIGHTS

Now over 60 years old, the case of the Lubbock lights is one of the oldest UFO cases on record. It began one night in August 1951 in Lubbock, Texas, USA, when three professors saw strange lights overhead. They were in a V-shape, and moving incredibly fast.

WE SAW THEM TOO!

When the witnesses reported their experience to the local paper, it turned out several other people had seen the lights, while others nearby had seen a huge, silent, flying wing-shaped object. The lights returned on several more nights, and a student named Carl Hart managed to photograph them.

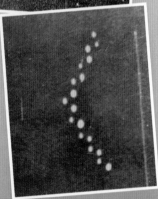

◀ Carl Hart's photographs of the Lubbock lights.

WHAT IS A UFO?

'UFO' stands for Unidentified Flying Object. This means it could be anything unrecognizable seen flying in the sky – from a faraway bird to a damaged weather balloon – and isn't necessarily spooky.

WHAT WERE THEY?

Several explanations have been given for the lights, but none of them make much sense.
• Mirages – lights from moving traffic or ships, refracted into the sky. But the lights were bright, making this unlikely.
• Secret aircraft – the USA did develop a 'flying wing', but if it was a real plane, why didn't it make a noise?
• Birds – ducks fly in a V-formation, but the lights seemed very fast.

UNEXPLAINED FACTOR

To this day, the Lubbock lights remain a huge mystery.

?????

▲ This real flying wing was tested by the US Air Force in the 1940s, but crashed.

WESTALL LANDING

Imagine a flying saucer landing next to your school! In April 1966, students and teachers of Westall School, Melbourne, Australia, witnessed a silvery-grey disc-shaped object fly over them, stop, drop down and land behind some trees.

◀ The UFO was described as round, with a bump on the top and smaller ones underneath.

GONE AGAIN

Pupils ran to see what the object was, but before they arrived it flew up into the air, and disappeared into the sky. It left a circle of flattened, heated grass. Some witnesses said they also saw some planes following the object as it flew off. There was lots of speculation about what the UFO was – a weather balloon, an air force training target, or a secret weapon.

SECRET ALIENS?

Despite many UFO sightings over the years, there's no proven evidence out in the open, that aliens exist and have been visiting us. Of course, this may be because they don't. But some people think governments and armed forces have covered the evidence up, to avoid a panic.

UNEXPLAINED FACTOR

Not only is this UFO still a mystery – it's also convincing as there were many witnesses.

❓❓❓❓❓

BELGIAN UFO WAVE

On the night of 29 November 1989, two Belgian police officers saw what looked like the lights of a huge, oddly shaped aircraft in the sky. Over the next few months, hundreds of people in Belgium saw the same thing!

SPACE TRIANGLE

Unlike a typical flying saucer, the Belgium UFOs were triangle-shaped, and seemed very large. Witnesses reported that they had a bright glowing light on each corner, as well as one in the middle, and that the lights could gradually change colour. The UFOs could change direction, move up and down or stop suddenly.

▲ The design of the mysterious craft, according to the many eyewitnesses.

UNEXPLAINED FACTOR

Although there's no proof, there were so many witnesses that this is hard to explain away.

❓❓❓❓

WHY FAKE IT?

People are fascinated by UFOs and the idea of aliens, and newspapers will pay well for a good photo. So people sometimes create fake UFO photos to try to make money or become famous.

HARD TO CATCH

On 30 March 1990, Belgium sent two F-16 fighter planes to chase the UFOs, but they kept slipping away. And when people tried to photograph them, the pictures came out blurred. One expert suggested this was because the UFOs gave out infra-red light which destroyed the pictures. There are some clear photos, but at least one of these is known to be a fake.

ROSWELL INCIDENT

There is no UFO incident more famous than the story that a flying saucer crashed at Roswell, New Mexico, in 1947. Reports claim there were three aliens on board, and that their bodies were recovered and examined. Could this really have been covered up?

CRASH ON THE RANCH

In July 1947, a worker at a ranch near Roswell reported finding debris. Staff from an army base collected the material, and reported that they had found a flying disk. But the next day, the crashed object was described as an experimental balloon, part of a secret US army surveillance test.

▼ A sign indicating the Roswell crash site.

UFO CRASH SITE

UFO Museum - 114 N. Main - Roswell

ALIEN AUTOPSY

In 1996 a film emerged that claimed to show an autopsy, or examination, of the body of a dead alien from Roswell. Later, though, the film was revealed to be a hoax.

UNEXPLAINED FACTOR

There are so many conflicting stories, fictional versions and hoaxes, its hard to say what really happened.

ROSWELL RUMOURS

The story died down until 1978, when a major who had been involved at the time claimed the balloon was a cover story, and the army really had found an alien flying saucer. More witnesses came forward to say they had seen the saucer, or even its inhabitants.

▲ This Roswell 'alien' was not real, but part of a hoaxed film.

BETTY AND BARNEY HILL

It must be scary enough seeing a UFO, but what about being taken inside one!? An American couple, Betty and Barney Hill, claimed this happened to them in 1961. They were driving late at night, when they saw a bright light in the sky and stopped to look.

MISSING TIME

The Hills remembered that as the light came closer, they saw that it was a saucer-shaped aircraft. They drove on. But their car began to make odd noises. The next thing they knew, they were much further down the road, and arrived home hours after they should have!

▼ The saucer the Hills said they saw looked like this.

STRANGE MEMORIES

Betty had dreams about her experience – including seeing strange alien books and a map of the stars. Later, the Hills went to see a hypnotist. Under hypnosis, they both remembered similar details about the saucer, aliens and sequence of events.

▲ Betty and Barney Hill.

GREY ALIENS

The Hill's story included greyish-looking aliens with large heads and huge dark eyes. These aliens, known as 'greys', feature in many UFO reports. However, some think this image is based on descriptions from old novels and TV shows.

UNEXPLAINED FACTOR

This case is famous, but sceptics think Betty could have imagined it and persuaded Barney.

🔲❓❓❓

chevrolet

ALLAGASH ABDUCTIONS

This alien abduction case dates from 1976, when four men were camping by a lake near Allagash, Maine, USA. One night they decided to go fishing. Out on the lake, they saw a glowing object in the sky.

WHERE ARE WE?

One of the men flashed his flashlight at the object, and it came nearer. Terrified, they paddled away, but a powerful light beam from the aircraft reached out and surrounded them. The next thing they remembered was being back on the shore, where their bonfire had burned down almost to nothing.

ALLAGASH SKETCHES

The four men in the Allagash incident met at art college, and all made detailed drawings of what happened to them.

▼ While fishing at night, four men witnessed a glowing orb in the sky.

UNEXPLAINED FACTOR

The men's story seemed genuine – but could they have been influenced by other abduction stories?

REMEMBERED EVENTS

After a head injury, one of the men remembered an alien making him lie on a table, and taking blood and skin samples from him. All the men had hypnosis and remembered similar events. And there were other reports of lights in the sky at the time.

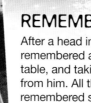

▲ The four Allagash abductees in later life.

LINDA NAPOLITANO

This case centres on Linda Napolitano, who claimed that in November 1989, she was 'floated' out of her 12th-floor apartment in New York City into a flying saucer that was hovering outside.

WHAT'S IN MY NOSE!?

Napolitano also claimed she had a strange bump near her nose, and went for an X-ray, which revealed a strange, small object implanted there! However, no one knows what this was or if it could have been hoaxed.

WITNESSES ON THE GROUND

As in other alien abduction cases, Linda remembered being examined by 'grey' aliens. It's hard to be sure if these 'remembered' events could have been imagined. But the case was unusual because other witnesses claimed they had seen the abduction, and the saucer hovering above the building.

UNEXPLAINED FACTOR

One of the best-documented and most convincing alien abduction reports.

RENDLESHAM FOREST UFO

The most famous British UFO case is the 1980 Rendlesham Forest incident of 1980. To this day, there is a UFO trail in the forest and markers showing where the UFO is said to have landed.

FOREST LIGHTS

In December 1980, American servicemen stationed at RAF Woodbridge, Suffolk, UK, reported a brightly lit triangular object hovering above the ground in nearby Rendlesham Forest. The next day, the base's deputy commander, Charles Halt, reported more lights, and also marks on the ground where the UFO was said to have landed.

▶ If you'd like to go UFO-spotting, try out Rendlesham Forest's UFO trail!

 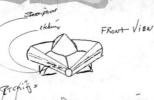

Top View   Inscription   etching   FRONT VIEW   etching   SIDE VIEW

UFO Trail

▶ Some of the witnesses later drew sketches of the flying machine.

CHARLES HALT

Deputy commander Charles Halt wrote an official memo about the sighting and declared he believed the UFO was a real alien craft. It's unusual for someone so senior and responsible to do this, and a reason why the case is so convincing.

UNEXPLAINED FACTOR

There is still no satifactory explanation for this incident.

LINEAR A

Cracking a code to decipher an ancient inscription is a theme in adventure films. But did you know undeciphered writings also exist in real life? Some still haven't been cracked – and one of the most famous is Linear A.

MINOAN LANGUAGE

Clay tablets with Linear A writing on them were first discovered in 1900, when archaeologist Arthur Evans was excavating the ancient palace of Knossos on the Greek island of Crete. This was the home of the ancient Minoan civilization, and Linear A is thought to represent the language they spoke between about 1800 BCE and 1450 BCE – dating back almost 3000 years.

SOUNDS OR SYMBOLS?

Before Linear A, ancient writing systems mainly used little pictures as symbols for different things. Linear A is different, as many of its symbols seems to stand for sounds and syllables, more like modern European scripts.

UNEXPLAINED FACTOR

After a century, we're still not much closer to decoding Linear A.

▲ Linear A has more than 100 different symbols or 'letters'.

RONGORONGO

Rongorongo is a set of symbols found on wooden objects on Easter Island (see page 33) in the 1800s. The symbols appear to be a writing system, and in the late 1800s, there were still people living on Easter Island who could understand what they said.

MINI PICTURES

Like some other writing systems, Rongorongo is made up of small pictures of human figures, plants and animals, and geometric shapes. There are at least 100 different symbols. The script is written in lines, and every second line is upside down. There are only a few examples of the script left, making it hard to decode.

▲ Can you spot different animals, plants and objects in the Rongorongo symbols?

UNEXPLAINED FACTOR

There's hardly any understanding so far of what these symbols mean!

HOW OLD IS RONGORONGO?

No one knows if Rongorongo is an old writing system, or one that was invented quite recently. Some experts think the islanders could have decided to develop their own writing after explorers from Europe first arrived on Easter Island in the 1700s, and the locals saw examples of their writing.

WHAT DOES 'RONGORONGO' MEAN?

The name Rongorongo comes from the islanders' name for the script. They called it kohau rongorongo, roughly meaning "lines for chanting". That could mean the rongorongo writings are songs or religious chants.

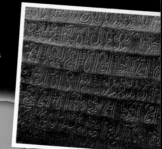

▲ A wooden tablet covered in Rongorongo symbols.

VOYNICH MANUSCRIPT

One of the most mysterious books in the world, the Voynich manuscript is a unique, handwritten, 600-year-old text that has defeated the best code-breakers in history.

WHERE DID IT COME FROM?

Carbon-dating suggests the book is not a hoax, but dates from the early 1400s. It only became well-known after a Polish book dealer, Wilfrid Voynich, bought it in Italy in 1912, and put it on public display. No one is sure where it came from or who wrote it.

CRACKING THE CODE

Computer analysis has shown the text has patterns that resemble the way real languages work. Professor Stephen Bax claims to have decoded some of the words based on knowledge of plants and constellations, but others disagree that he's right. The challenge continues!

◄ The manuscript was found by rare book dealer Wilfrid Voynich.

▼ The strange text and pictures of the Voynich manuscript.

WHAT'S IN IT?

The manuscript contains over 300,000 words. There are hundreds of colour illustrations, many showing stars and planets, maps, buildings, medicine bottles, and strange plants that cannot be identified as real plant species.

UNEXPLAINED FACTOR

A bizarre, bonkers, but beautifully illustrated, total mystery!

ROHONC CODEX

This baffling book appeared in Hungary in the 1800s. It is written in an ancient-looking language that no one has ever decoded and illustrated with drawings of battles, buildings and everyday scenes.

LOTS OF THEORIES

Many people have tried to decipher the Rohonc codex and they've come up with all kinds of ideas. Some say the language in it is like ancient Hungarian; others say it's more like Indian, Romanian or Turkish. The language has an unusual alphabet with over 200 letters – most alphabets have far fewer – but it's thought some of these could be symbols for people and place names.

IS IT A FAKE?

The paper the codex is written on dates from the 1500s, but it could have been written later. One theory is that a forger, Sámuel Literáti Nemes, created the manuscript as a hoax.

▲ Text and illustrations from the Rohonc codex.

UNEXPLAINED FACTOR

The meaning of the Rohonc codex is disputed, but still very unclear.

WOW! SIGNAL

If aliens exist, why don't they contact us? Maybe they have! For decades, humans have been listening for messages from other planets, a project known as SETI – the Search for Extra-Terrestrial Intelligence.

▼ The telescope that detected the Wow! signal is called the Big Ear. It works by reflecting radio waves into two small receivers.

WAS IT ALIENS?

The Wow! signal can't be explained as coming from anywhere on Earth, as it was the wrong frequency. Even though scientists scanned the same point in space over and over again, it was never detected again. If it was a message from aliens, they only sent one!

WOW!

In 1977, a volunteer named Jerry Ehman was checking the results from a telescope in Ohio, USA, that was scanning the sky for possible signals. Suddenly, Ehman spotted something very different – an extremely strong radio signal coming from one point in space. He was so amazed, he circled the signal and wrote "Wow!" next to it.

▼ The printout used the numbers 1–9, then the letters A–Z for even stronger signals. The Wow! signal was very strong, as it goes up to the letter U.

UNEXPLAINED FACTOR

If the signal wasn't from aliens, it must have been from something we don't yet understand.

? ? ? ? ?

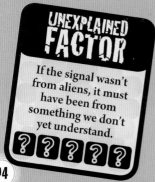

94

MOON ILLUSION

If you see the Moon when it is close to the horizon, it looks much bigger than when it is high in the sky. People have noticed this since ancient times. But it's actually just an illusion – the Moon illusion!

NO CHANGE

If you measure the Moon by holding up a ruler at arm's length, you'll see its size is actually exactly the same, wherever it is. Photographs of the moon moving up and down the sky also prove that it does not change in size.

◄ A Moon near the horizon looks larger than a moon high in the sky.

SO WHICH IS IT?

No one knows. Despite being able to send spacecraft to the Moon, we still haven't managed to work out the Moon illusion once and for all!

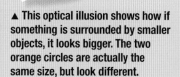

▲ This optical illusion shows how if something is surrounded by smaller objects, it looks bigger. The two orange circles are actually the same size, but look different.

UNEXPLAINED FACTOR

We do have some explanations. We just don't know which one, if either, is right!

MOON MYSTERY

There are two explanations so far:

• When the Moon is high, it's surrounded by a vast area of sky, making it look smaller. But when it's low, we see it next to smaller items like trees, so it looks bigger.

• We know that if we see birds or clouds near the horizon, they are usually much further away than when they are overhead. Our brain decides that the Moon must be further away too, and in order for it to appear the same size, must actually be much bigger.

PLACEBO EFFECT

Pills and treatments that contain no actual medicine are called placebos. Amazingly, doctors have discovered that can they actually make people feel better. This is called the 'placebo effect'.

HOW DOES IT WORK?

Scientists don't know exactly how the placebo effect works, but there are different theories.

• The act of listening to a patient, and giving them something, can help them feel calm and may improve their symptoms.

• If a patient expects a medicine to help them, this may stimulate the brain to help the body heal itself.

UNEXPLAINED FACTOR

It is definitely something to do with the brain – but how it happens is not known.

? ? ? ?

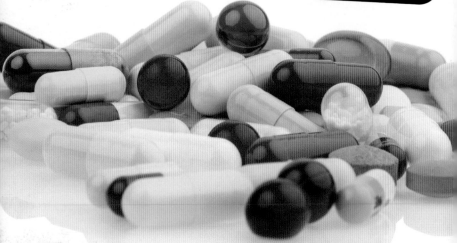

IN THE KNOW

Placebos don't just work when the patient thinks they are being given real medicine. Incredibly, they can also work even when the patient knows they are getting a placebo! No one knows why this is.

▲ A convincing-looking packet of pills may help you feel better, even if they are not real medicine.

• If you think you are taking medicine, you may perceive pain or other symptoms differently, and decide they aren't as bad, even if that's not the case.

DÉJÀ VU

You're in a town you've never visited before, or talking to someone you've never met before, and you get the WEIRDEST feeling you're experiencing things for the second time! You're experiencing déjà vu – French for 'already seen'.

PAST LIFE?

Some people have said déjà vu is proof that humans have actually been here before – that we live our lives over and over again. This is a belief held by some religions, and is known as reincarnation.

NO DÉJÀ VU FOR YOU?

There are some people who say they've never had déjà vu. However, it's most common between the ages of 15–25, so if you haven't had it yet, you might before long!

UNEXPLAINED FACTOR

It's quite spooky when it's happening, but there could be a simple explanation.

OR BRAIN GLITCH?

Scientists say it's likely that déjà vu happens when something goes a bit wrong in your brain. You don't actually experience events around you at the moment they happen. It takes a moment for your brain to piece everything together and make sense of it. Maybe it sometimes 'replays' the same bit, making it feel like an old memory.

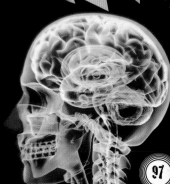

WHY DO WE YAWN?

What makes you yawn? Most people yawn when they're tired or bored, or just after they wake up. Another thing that can make you yawn is seeing someone else yawn. Although it's common, scientists aren't sure why we yawn, or why it's so catching.

COULD IT BE...?

Here are two of the ideas experts have come up with to explain why we yawn:

• Stretching – yawning stretches the mouth, throat and neck, keeping them in good condition and preventing cramp.

• Cooling – opening the mouth wide helps to cool down your brain, making it work faster, and making you feel more awake. Scientists have found if your brain is already cool, you tend to yawn less.

UNEXPLAINED FACTOR

Still unexplained, but there are lots of possible reasons for yawning.

▼ Some people think a yawn gives you extra oxygen, helping to wake you up.

INFECTIOUS YAWNING

Why do we 'catch' yawns from other people? One reason could be that when humans are in a group, if one is getting sleepy or distracted, they probably all are. Group yawning helps everyone to become more alert. In prehistoric times, this could have been useful for avoiding danger.

DID YOU KNOW?
Many animals yawn too, and dogs can 'catch' yawns from their human owners!

WHY DO WE DREAM?

While you're asleep, you may experience all kinds of strange things – from flying, to having your teeth fall out. Yet dreams also feature familiar things too, like your family or friends. What's going on?

BUSY BRAIN

One explanation for dreams is that the 'sensible' part of your brain is switched off for the night. That's why you don't realize you're dreaming, and accept the weird things that happen. It could also allow your brain to explore your deepest fears and hopes, which you stop yourself from thinking about during the day. This could explain why people have lots of dreams about important exams they have coming up, for example.

POINTLESS DREAMS

Another theory is that dreams serve no purpose at all – they just happen because of signals in the brain firing off at random when we're asleep.

▼ As you dream, the brain sorts through all the things you have recently experienced.

UNEXPLAINED FACTOR

Scientists don't all agree on the reasons for dreaming, but they have lots of good theories.

ORIGIN OF LIFE

It's one of the biggest questions of all. Earth is the only planet we know of that has living things on it – so how did that happen? How did the first living things develop, and where did they come from?

CHEMICAL MIXTURE

Most scientists think life on Earth started when chemicals reacted with each other to make more complex chemicals. These formed units that could copy themselves and developed into living cells. Where did this happen? Some think it was in a liquid 'primordial soup', in a pool or a hot spring. Others think it is more likely to have happened in clay, or in rocks underground.

▼ Life could have formed in pools or springs like these, over 3 billion years ago.

DO IT YOURSELF

If life appeared from a mixture of chemicals, it should be possible to make it happen again. But scientists have never managed to do this.

UNEXPLAINED FACTOR

We don't know where we, or all the other living things on Earth, came from.

?????

LIFE FROM SPACE

Another interesting idea says life first arrived in the Earth from somewhere else in space, in the form of bacteria-like cells carried to our planet by a comet or asteroid. If that's true, it means we're all aliens!

▲ Under the microscope, the earliest life on Earth might have looked a bit like this.

LIFE ON OTHER PLANETS

Are we alone in the universe... or could there be other life forms on other planets? Though there are lots of UFO reports, we still don't have any clear evidence that aliens exist.

HI, IT'S US!

Several messages have been sent into space to let any aliens know we are here. The Arecibo message in 1974 was a radio signal containing information about humans, DNA and the solar system.

EXOPLANET EXPLOSION

In the 1980s, astronomers began to detect planets orbiting around other stars in the sky. Scientists call them exoplanets, or 'outside' planets. A few of these are similar to Earth in their temperature and habitat, meaning life could survive there.

IS ANYBODY OUT THERE?

If aliens are out there, we would expect to get messages from them – especially radio signals, which can travel long distances across empty space. In fact, we've only ever detected a few unexplained signals, such as the Wow! signal (see page 94).

▶ What might aliens or their worlds look like? Sci-fi books and movies have explored this, but no one knows for sure.

UNEXPLAINED FACTOR

If we ever find the answer to this massive mystery, it could change everything!

MONARCH MIGRATIONS

Monarch butterflies fly up to 4000 kilometres (2500 miles) from their summer home in Canada and the northern USA, to spend winter in Mexico, Florida or southern California. This is amazing enough, but there's a bigger mystery!

HOW DO THEY KNOW!?

Every autumn, monarch butterflies fly back to the same southern overwintering spots. But the monarchs that do this are not the ones that left in the spring! After setting off from their winter home, they mate and lay eggs, which hatch into caterpillars, which become new monarchs. This happens about four times over. So the butterflies that set off back to the south are the great-great-grandchildren of the ones that left.

Scientists think they find their way thanks to a combination of factors – navigating by the position of the Sun, sensing the Earth's magnetic field, and possibly sniffing out a scent left behind in their winter home by previous generations.

BUTTERFLY BRAIN

The monarchs' migrations are especially amazing as they have teeny, weeny brains – about the size of the ball in the tip of a ballpoint pen!

▲ Monarch butterflies roost on the trees after their long journey.

◄ Migration routes.

UNEXPLAINED FACTOR

A major mystery in the insect world.

PERIODICAL CICADAS

Cicadas are bug-like insects that spend a few years as nymphs (babies) living underground. Every year, some emerge as adults to mate and lay eggs. But one group, the periodical cicadas, are much stranger.

17 YEARS UNDERGROUND

Periodical cicadas live longer than any other insect. Some spend 13 years underground as nymphs, and some spend 17 years. But the strangest thing is that huge groups of them live their life cycles together, all emerging at the same time. So, after 13 (or 17) years in the soil, with no sign of a cicada anywhere, suddenly thousands of them will appear, covering trees and gardens, and creating a deafening noise.

▼ An adult periodical cicada.

Scientists don't know how the cicadas 'count' how many years they have been underground, or signal to each other to all emerge at once. It's also a mystery how the unusual 13- and 17-year life cycles developed.

PERIODICAL PRIME NUMBERS

Thirteen and seventeen are prime numbers – numbers that can only be divided by themselves and 1. Why do the cicadas use these numbers? It could be because it makes other animals' life cycles unlikely to coincide with them, helping the cicadas to avoid predators.

UNEXPLAINED FACTOR

Scientists are still studying periodical cicadas to try to find out more about them.

GRAVITY

Everyone understands gravity – don't they? It's what pulls you down to the ground when you jump off a wall. It holds us, and everything around us, onto the Earth, and stops us floating away. We're so used to gravity, we don't think about how weird it is.

▼ Gravity pulls down towards the Earth.

PULLING POWER

One way to describe gravity is as a force that pulls objects towards each other. It's not just the Earth that has gravity – everything does. We just feel it most from the Earth, because it's the biggest object in the area. The gravity of the Earth and the Moon also pull on each other. That means the force of gravity can pull across empty space – a vacuum. How? No one really knows!

UNEXPLAINED FACTOR

Some everyday phenomena are actually the biggest scientific mysteries of all.

▲ The Sun's gravity holds the planets in orbit around it.

▲ Albert Einstein.

EINSTEIN'S IDEA

The great scientist Albert Einstein said that rather than being a force, gravity happens because matter – objects like the Earth – bend time and space, making objects fall together.

MATTER

Matter means stuff – all the stuff around us, that everything is made of. Trees, rocks, toys, clothes, food, and living things, including humas, are all made of matter. Though it's a basic part of our existence, science cannot yet explain it!

MATTER AND ENERGY

Matter can be turned into energy, and vice versa. One way to imagine matter is as a type of energy. The movements of the particles are what give objects and substances their 3D, 'real' qualities.

Electrons zooming around the nucleus.

Nucleus filled with protons and neutrons.

▲ A typical atom.

WHAT IS MATTER MADE FROM?

We know matter is made up of different types of units called atoms. Atoms are made of even tinier bits called protons, neutrons and electrons. Protons and neutrons are made of minuscule subatomic particles, called quarks. But now it gets a bit weird. Scientists think that the tiniest particles, such as quarks and electrons, actually don't take up any space at all. They have mass, meaning they weigh something – but no size! That would actually mean there is no solid matter.

UNEXPLAINED FACTOR

Freaky as it may seem, we don't know what everything is actually made of.

TIME

It's hard to imagine life without time. School days, baking cakes, playing a football match and a million other things would make no sense without it. If someone asks you, "what time is it?", you know exactly what they mean, and how to find out the answer. But if you try explaining what time actually is, you'll find it's not easy!

ONE-WAY STREET

You can see time as a dimension, in which events happen one after another. But time only goes in one direction – from past to future. We can't go back in time, but it's hard to explain why. Some say that time is a real thing, and part of the natural universe. Others say it is an illusion resulting from the way we perceive things. Because it's impossible to 'stand outside' time, it's very hard to see how it works.

SPACETIME

Top scientist Albert Einstein thought that space and time are actually both part of one concept, which he called spacetime. Einstein showed that if objects move at different speeds relative to each other, time goes at different speeds for them. This has now been proved – clocks on orbiting spacecraft run slightly slower than on Earth, for example.

◀ Time is important in our daily lives, but what is it really?

UNEXPLAINED FACTOR

Perhaps the hardest thing of all to explain.

CONSCIOUSNESS

Consciousness means being aware of what's going on in your head. In other words, thinking and *knowing* that you are thinking. We all experience this. We have a 'life of the mind' where we can weigh up decisions, and think about how we feel. We're used to it. But it's actually very hard to explain.

BRAIN BITS

Your brain is made up of a tangle of brain cells, or neurons, with tree-like branches at the ends. Each branch touches the branches of other cells, forming pathways that signals can zoom along. Thinking happens as signals travel along different pathways.

But how can signals in a network of cells add up to 'thoughts' such as "I can't wait to go camping!", or "I can't remember where I was supposed to meet my friend?". Scientists are still trying to work this out.

THE BIG DEBATE

There are two opposing views on consciousness. Some people think only the brain exists, and somehow creates thoughts and the 'mind'. Others say the mind, or soul, is separate from the body and is not a physical thing. What do you think?

▲ There are billions of brain cells in your brain, and gazillions of possible pathways between them.

UNEXPLAINED FACTOR

Scientists have done, and still do, many experiments to understand consciousness.

◄ You think all the time... but what is really happening?

INDEX

A

aircraft 36, 72–73, 78–79, 82
alien abductions 73, 86–88
aliens 30, 31, 37, 49, 73, 83, 85–88, 94, 101
Allagash abductions 87
animal ghosts 65
animal rain 45
Antikythera mechanism 38
Atlantis 28
atoms 105

B

Baghdad batteries 39
Baigong pipes 37
ball lightning 42
Ballygally Castle 67
batteries 39
Belgian UFO wave 84
Bermuda Triangle 20, 73
Bigfoot 9
books, mysterious 92–93
Borley Rectory 56
brain science 51, 76, 77, 96, 97, 98, 99, 107

Brown Lady of Raynham Hall 57
bunyips 12
Burke and Hare 68

C

caecilians 15
cicadas, periodical 103
cloud formations 43
comets 44, 100
consciousness 107
Costa Rica stone spheres 30
crop circles 49
cryptids 8–19
Cuzco 33

D

déjà vu 97
Dingonek 14
Diprotodon 12
disappearances 20, 72–75
dreaming 99

E

Earhart, Amelia 72
earthquake lights 46
earthquakes 28, 33, 46
Easter Island 33, 91
Edinburgh Vaults 68

Eilean Mòr mystery 75
Einstein, Albert 104, 106
electric eels 16
energy 105
ESP (Extra-Sensory Perception) 54
exoplanets 101

F

Faces of Belmez 70
Faces of SS Watertown 71
fireballs 42, 47
Flight 19 73
Flores Man 17
Flying Dutchman 63
flying saucer clouds 43
footprints, giant 23

G

Gage, Phineas 76
ghosts and hauntings 48, 56–71
giants 23
Glamis Castle 66
Göbekli Tepe 27
gravity 104

H

Hill, Betty and Barney 86
hippopotamuses 81
hums 22

K

Knighton Gorges Manor 69
Koepcke, Juliane 79
kraken 13

L

Lake Champlain monster 11
levitation 52
life on other planets 93, 101
life, origin of 100
lights 46–48, 82
Lincoln, Abraham 62
Linear A writing 90
Loch Ness monster 10
Lubbock lights 82

M

manatees 19
Maoi 33
Mary Celeste 74
matter 104, 105
mermaids 19

migrations 102
Minhocão 15
mirages 48, 63, 82
monarch butterflies 102
Mongolian death worm 16
Moon illusion 95
Mothman 18
Muamba, Fabrice 77
Myrtles Plantation 58

N

Naga fireballs 47
Nan Madol 24
Napolitano, Linda 88
Nazca lines 31

O

Oakville blobs 40
Okene, Harrison 80
orang pendek 17
orangutans 17
out-of-body experiences 50
Owlman 18

P

Paulding light 48
placebo effect 96
plesiosaurs 10
psychokinesis 52
Pyramids of Giza 34

R

Racetrack Playa 21
red rain of Kerala 44
reincarnation 97
remote viewing 54
Rendlesham Forest UFO 89
Rohonc codex 93
Rongorongo 91
Rose Hall 59
Roswell incident 85

S

sabre-tooth tigers 14
Saksaywaman 32
Santorini 28
Saqqara Bird 36
Sasquatch 9
SETI (Search for Extra-Terrestrial Intelligence) 94, 101
ships and boats 20, 54, 63, 74, 80
Skeleton Lake 25
sliders 51
snakes 16
spacetime 106
Sphinx 35
spontaneous human combustion 55
squid 13
Stanley Hotel 60

star jelly 41
stone circles 26, 27
stone monuments 24,
  26, 27, 29, 34
stone spheres 30
stone statues 33, 35
stone walls 32
Stonehenge 24, 26
stones, sailing 21
survival stories 76–81

T

Taos hum 22
telepathy 53, 54
Templer, Paul 81
Theatre Royal ghost
  64
time 106
Titanic 54
Tower of London
  ghosts 65

U

UFOs 43, 46, 82–89, 101
underwater structures
  28–29

V

Voynich manuscript 92
Vulovic, Vesna 78

W

waterspouts 45
Westall landing 83
White House 62
Winchester Mystery
  House 61
worms 15, 16
WOW! signal 94, 101
writing systems,
  undeciphered 90–93

Y

yawning 98
Yeti 8, 9
Yonaguni Monument
  29

PICTURE CREDITS

The publisher thanks the following agencies for their kind permission to use their images.

Key: t=top, a=above, l=lower, b=below

Alamy, pp.5bl/c, 11t, 29, 38t/b, 41t, 46b, 49t, 50t, 52t, 55t, 56t, 57, 60b, 64, 65cl, 67, 68, 70, 71, 75, 76, 77t/b, 78, 85b, 86t/b, 89t/br, 90b, 92cl

Bucklin, Linda, Shutterstock.com, p.28

Caetano, Carlos, Shutterstock.com, p.99

Copyright 2014 Melita Curphy MissMonster.com, pp.4t, 14

Corbis, pp.9br, 26, 30, 35b, 47t, 80tr, 82t/c/b, 97t

Courtesy of Charles Foltz, p.87bl

Courtesy of okc.net, pp.5tr, 19l

Courtesy of Teeta Moss, p.58bl

CT Snow, Wikipedia, p.25

Dalmingo, Shutterstock.com, p.104bl

DarkOne, Shutterstock.com, p.34bl

Deliyergiyev, Maksym, Shutterstock.com, p.44br

Digital Storm, Shutterstock.com, p.97br

Dreamstime, pp.1tr, 17br, 22, 25, 27br, 33bl, 40bl, 43bl, 46t, 47t, 54b, 60t, 61t, 62, 63, 65tl/br, 66, 81, 83, 87c, 88, 95, 96, 98b, 102b, 107

FPLA, pp.4bl, 15

Funkyfrogstock, Shutterstock.com, p.51

Germanskydiver, Shutterstock.com, p.104t

Getty Images, pp.9t, 11t, 27, 31, 61br, 72t/b, 73, 74, 79b, 85

Hunta, Aleksandr, Shutterstock.com, p.16t

J.S. Henrardi, Wikipedia, p.84

Jorgensen - Jorgo, Ryan, Shutterstock.com, p.45t

Khandelwal, Sudhir, www.himalayanadventurer.blogspot.in, p.25cl

Kollidas, Shutterstock.com, p.104bc

KUCO, Shutterstock.com, p.45bl

Liquid Productions, LLC, Shutterstock.com, p.19b

Lolloj, Shutterstock.com, p.53

Mikenorton, Shutterstock.com, p.21

National Library of Australia, p.12

NCG, Shutterstockc.om, p.102cr

Orsillo, Bob, Shutterstock.com, pp.4br, 10b

Photoshot, pp.41bl, 55b

Pius Lee, Shutterstock.com, p.35

Press Association, p.79t

Radojko, Zeljko, Shutterstock.com, p.44t

Rafcha, Shutterstock.com, p.33

Rihardzz, Shutterstock.com, p.54t

Sarah2, Shutterstock.com, p.40t

Science Photo Library, pp.3, 16cr, 31cr, 42t/b, 43t, 94t, 100t

Sommerland, Atelier, Shutterstock.com, p.19tr

Terriberry, Mary, Shutterstock.com, p.103

TopFoto, p.39t

Urban Walnut, Wikipedia, p.59t/b

Vakhrushev, Pavel, Shutterstock.com, p.47b

VanderWolf Images, Shutterstock.com, p.37b

VILevi, Shutterstock.com, p.51b

Vitmark, Shutterstock.com, p.33

Wikipedia, pp.58t, 69

WitR, Shutterstock.com, p.34

Yury, Kisialiou, Shutterstock.com, p.20

Ziganshin, Albert, Shutterstock.com, pp.1br, 101

While every effort has been made to credit contributors, Quarto would like to apologize should there have been any omissions or errors – and would be pleased to make the appropriate correction for future editions of the book.